-2

D1716414

Writing the Critical Essay

Gun Control

An OPPOSING **VIEWPOINTS**® Guide

Lauri S. Friedman, *Book Editor*

OPPOSING
VIEWPOINTS®
SERIES

GREENHAVEN PRESS
A part of Gale, Cengage Learning

GALE
CENGAGE Learning™

Detroit • New York • San Francisco • New Haven, Conn • Waterville, Maine • London

Christine Nasso, *Publisher*
Elizabeth Des Chenes, *Managing Editor*

For more information, contact:
Greenhaven Press
27500 Drake Rd.
Farmington Hills, MI 48331-3535
Or you can visit our Internet site at gale.cengage.com

For product information and technology assistance, contact us at

Gale Customer Support, 1-800-877-4253
For permission to use material from this text or product, submit all requests online at
www.cengage.com/permissions

Further permissions questions can be emailed to permissionrequest@cengage.com

Articles in Greenhaven Press anthologies are often edited for length to meet page requirements. In addition, original titles of these works are changed to clearly present the main thesis and to explicitly indicate the author's opinion. Every effort is made to ensure that Greenhaven Press accurately reflects the original intent of the authors. Every effort has been made to trace the owners of copyrighted material.

Cover image copyright 9387388673, 2008. Used under license from Shutterstock.com.

LIBRARY OF CONGRESS CATALOGING-IN-PUBLICATION DATA

Gun control / Lauri S. Friedman, book editor.
      p. cm. — (Writing the critical essay : an opposing viewpoints guide)
   Includes bibliographical references and index.
   ISBN 978-0-7377-4264-0 (hardcover)
   1. Gun control—United States. 2. Firearms and crime—United States. 3. Essay—
Authorship. I. Friedman, Lauri S.
   HV7436.G8634 2008
   363.330973—dc22
                                                                        2008037874

Printed in the United States of America
  2 3 4 5 6 7 12 11 10 09

CONTENTS

Examining the state of writing and how it is taught in the United States was the official purpose of the National Commission on Writing in America's Schools and Colleges. The commission, made up of teachers, school administrators, business leaders, and college and university presidents, released its first report in 2003. "Despite the best efforts of many educators," commissioners argued, "writing has not received the full attention it deserves." Among the findings of the commission was that most fourth-grade students spent less than three hours a week writing, that three-quarters of high school seniors never receive a writing assignment in their history or social studies classes, and that more than 50 percent of first-year students in college have problems writing error-free papers. The commission called for a "cultural sea change" that would increase the emphasis on writing for both elementary and secondary schools. These conclusions have made some educators realize that writing must be emphasized in the curriculum. As colleges are demanding an ever-higher level of writing proficiency from incoming students, schools must respond by making students more competent writers. In response to these concerns, the SAT, an influential standardized test used for college admissions, required an essay for the first time in 2005.

Books in the Writing the Critical Essay: An Opposing Viewpoints Guide series use the patented Opposing Viewpoints format to help students learn to organize ideas and arguments and to write essays using common critical writing techniques. Each book in the series focuses on a particular type of essay writing—including expository, persuasive, descriptive, and narrative—that students learn while being taught both the five-paragraph essay as well as longer pieces of writing that have an opinionated focus. These guides include everything necessary to help students research, outline, draft, edit, and ultimately write successful essays across the curriculum, including essays for the SAT.

Using Opposing Viewpoints

This series is inspired by and builds upon Greenhaven Press's acclaimed Opposing Viewpoints series. As in the parent series, each book in the Writing the Critical Essay series focuses on a timely and controversial social issue that provides lots of opportunities for creating thought-provoking essays. The first section of each volume begins with a brief introductory essay that provides context for the opposing viewpoints that follow. These articles are chosen for their accessibility and clearly stated views. The thesis of each article is made explicit in the article's title and is accentuated by its pairing with an opposing or alternative view. These essays are both models of persuasive writing techniques and valuable research material that students can mine to write their own informed essays. Guided reading and discussion questions help lead students to key ideas and writing techniques presented in the selections.

The second section of each book begins with a preface discussing the format of the essays and examining characteristics of the featured essay type. Model five-paragraph and longer essays then demonstrate that essay type. The essays are annotated so that key writing elements and techniques are pointed out to the student. Sequential, step-by-step exercises help students construct and refine thesis statements; organize material into outlines; analyze and try out writing techniques; write transitions, introductions, and conclusions; and incorporate quotations and other researched material. Ultimately, students construct their own compositions using the designated essay type.

The third section of each volume provides additional research material and writing prompts to help the student. Additional facts about the topic of the book serve as a convenient source of supporting material for essays. Other features help students go beyond the book for their research. Like other Greenhaven Press books, each book in the Writing the Critical Essay series includes bibliographic listings of relevant periodical articles, books, Web sites, and organizations to contact.

Writing the Critical Essay: An Opposing Viewpoints Guide will help students master essay techniques that can be used in any discipline.

The Meaning of the Second Amendment

The Second Amendment of the U.S. Constitution is one of the shortest in all of the Bill of Rights. It simply states, "A well-regulated Militia, being necessary to the security of a free State, the right of the people to keep and bear Arms, shall not be infringed." The Second Amendment was written at the time of America's birth and reflected the colonists' deep and necessary commitment to self-defense. After all, it was the spirit of self-defense that helped the new citizens of the United States win their freedom from the British. Granting the people the right to keep and bear arms, therefore, was seen as essential to preventing another colonizer from exerting influence over the young nation, and also to prevent government forces from ever getting the upper hand over the citizenry.

Yet volumes have been written about the meaning of these twenty-seven short words and what they offer Americans. By some accounts, the Second Amendment grants individual Americans the right to own a gun. By other interpretations, the Second Amendment grants American citizens the right to have a militia or army that can own guns in order to protect them but does not guarantee the right of private individuals to own guns, and is subject to government regulation. The meaning of the Second Amendment is at the heart of all other controversies related to gun control, including whether or not Americans have the right to own guns, which guns they should be allowed to own, how they should be allowed to use their guns, and what restrictions, if any, should be placed on gun ownership.

For those Americans who believe in the right to gun ownership, the values and ideas enshrined in the Second Amendment are as valid and appropriate today as they were at the beginning of American history. In fact, some argue that due to a less personalized society, an increase in violence and depravity, more dangerous technology, and a breakdown of societal values and responsibility, the right to keep a gun may be even more critical than ever. Nationally syndicated commentator Mike Gallagher is one person who argued this point after the brutal slaying of thirty-two people at Virginia Tech on April 16, 2007. "There is only one way that an evil monster who is intent on killing as many people as he can will be stopped," writes Gallagher. "It's called the Second Amendment. Somewhere along the way, we've lost sight of allowing people to have this fundamental right. The very reason people desperately want to protect the right to keep and bear arms is so they can continue to defend and protect themselves—and others."[1] People like Gallagher argue that the best way to deal with problems of violence, crime, and particularly the newer phenomenon of school and work-place shootings is to encourage Americans to embrace their constitutionally protected right to self-defense. As his colleague Michelle Malkin has put it, a safer America "begins with renewing a culture of self-defense—mind, spirit and body. It begins with two words: Fight back."[2]

Yet for many other Americans, it seems like a contra-diction in terms for Americans to seek safety and peace by arming themselves to the teeth. Some of these Americans reject the suggestion that the Second Amendment was ever supposed to grant private individuals the right to own guns. They point to the phrase "well-regulated militia" to show that the authors of the Constitution intended for Americans to have the right to be protected by an armed militia, or army, and that such a group was to be regulated by the gun control laws set down by the government.

And even when Americans believe that the Second Amendment grants them the right to own a gun, it doesn't necessarily mean they oppose gun control. In fact, many Americans who support gun control laws believe that guns—and the society that has access to them—have changed so much since the Framers adopted the Second Amendment that the right to keep and bear arms can no longer be reasonably applied the way it was

once meant. Indeed, when the Second Amendment was adopted more than two hundred years ago, dangerous weapons such as handguns and semi-automatic weapons hadn't yet been invented. The guns the authors of the Constitution knew were rifles that shot musket balls, which, due to their primitive design, took a long time to load and were incapable of doing the kind of damage that the sleek, rapid-fire weapons of the modern world are. As writer Max Castro has put it, "The right to bear arms made sense in the 18th Century to provide for the common defense and afford citizens a guarantee against the encroachment of absolute monarchs. But today we don't rely on a militia to defend the country, and tyranny would involve a monopoly of media, not muskets."[3]

The suggestion that gun ownership is no longer appropriate for contemporary society seems further justified when one considers the mass shootings, homicides, suicides, and accidental deaths that claim the lives of thirty thousand people each year. In the eyes of gun control advocates, guns are simply unsafe products, and the government has

The Second Amendment, which grants "the right of the people to keep and bear arms," is a highly controversial topic in America today.

Marchers at a gun control rally at Prospect Park in Brooklyn, New York, believe that gun control in modern America is a necessity.

a responsibility to protect its citizens from them. Indeed, the United States is a place in which a tainted bag of pet food or a lead-laced toy is reason enough to pull thousands of products from store shelves if they pose a public safety hazard. Columnist Elayne Boosler has suggested that guns should be treated the same way. To make the point, she compares guns to apples, arguing that if tens of thousands of people a year were sickened and died after eating apples, it is likely the government would take swift action and regulate apple sales harshly. Says Boosler, "There wouldn't be an apple left on the shelves or in the homes of this country until apples could be made safe. Screw your 'constitutional right' to have an apple, there is something called the 'greater good.'"[4]

Whether the Second Amendment actually gives private citizens the right to bear arms or whether that right is to be reserved exclusively for members of a "militia" was debated before the Supreme Court in 2008 in the landmark case *District of Columbia v. Heller*. In that case, the Court held that the Second Amendment does indeed protect an individual's right to possess a firearm for private use. The case was notable because it was the first time in U.S. history it had been clarified that the right to keep and bear arms was specifically the right of private individuals. However, the Court did not rule to what extent the Second Amendment grants Americans this right, or what type of guns this right covers.

This topic, as well as whether gun control increases or decreases crime and violence in America, are among the topics explored in *Writing the Critical Essay: An Opposing Viewpoints Guide: Gun Control*. Model essays and thought-provoking writing exercises help readers develop their own opinions and write their own cause-and-effect essays on this timeless and impassioned subject.

Notes

1. Mike Gallagher, "Preventing Another Massacre," Townhall.com, April 20, 2007. http://mikegallagher.townhall.com/columnists/MikeGallagher/2007/04/20/preventing_another_massacre.

2. Michelle Malkin, "Wanted: A Culture of Self-Defense," Townhall.com, April 18, 2007.

3. Max Castro, "It's Time to Repeal the Second Amendment," *Miami Herald,* May 24, 2000.

4. Elayne Boosler, "We Are Getting Tired of Prying Your Guns Out of Your Cold Dead Hands," Huffington Post.com, April 18, 2007. http://www.huffingtonpost.com/elayne-boosler/we-are-getting-tired-of-p_b_46196.html.

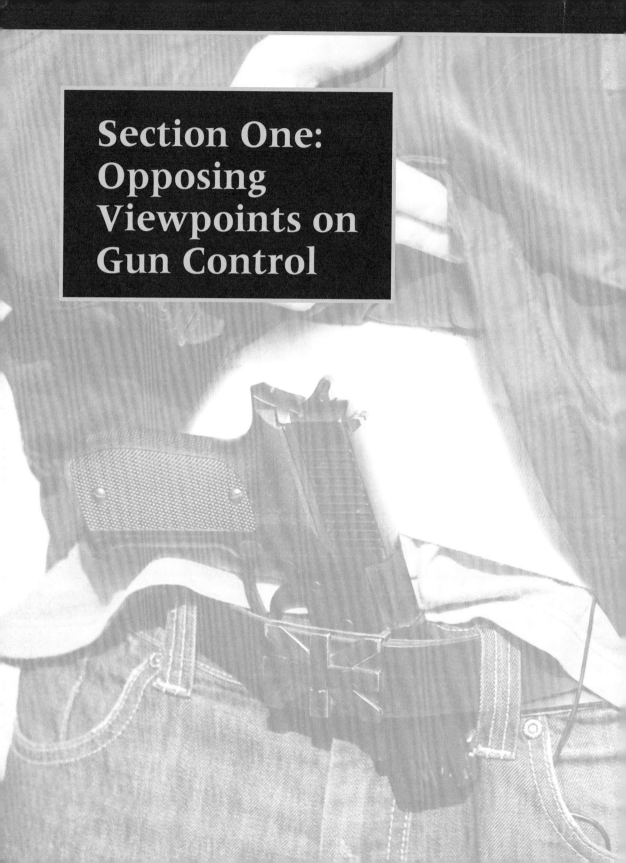

Section One: Opposing Viewpoints on Gun Control

Guns Keep Americans Safe

Viewpoint One

Don B. Kates and Carol Hehmeyer

In the following essay Don B. Kates and Carol Hehmeyer argue that owning guns keeps people safe. They contend that most guns are owned by law-abiding citizens who use them to thwart crime, including murder. The authors cite statistics from Europe showing that nations with high gun ownership have low murder rates, and countries with low gun ownership have high murder rates. They explain this phenomenon with the assertion that, when criminals know a nearby person is armed, they are less likely to commit a crime. Kates and Hehmeyer conclude that gun ownership keeps crime rates low and that attempts to disarm gun owners will only benefit criminals.

Kates is a lawyer and criminologist associated with the Independent Institute in Oakland, California. Hehmeyer is a retired San Francisco deputy district attorney.

Consider the following questions:

1. In what way is the African American community proof of the argument that more guns do not equal more murder, in the authors' opinion?
2. What is the correlation between gun ownership and murder in Germany, Austria, Luxembourg, and Hungary, as reported by Kates and Hehmeyer?
3. What effect do the authors say gun control laws have on law-abiding gun owners?

Don B. Kates and Carol Hehmeyer, "Nation's Rates of Private Gun Ownership Do Not Correlate to Rates Of Murder," *Daily Journal*, August 6, 2007. Reproduced by permission.

Many people think that nations with more firearms will have more murder and that banning firearms will reduce murder and other violence. This canard does not comport, however, with criminological research in the U.S. or elsewhere.

Gun Ownership Correlates with Lower Murder Rates

An extensive study . . . recently published [by Kates] with Canadian criminologist Gary Mauser confirms the negative results of two large-scale international studies over the past 15 years. These studies compared data from a large number of nations around the world. There were no instances of nations with high gun ownership having higher murder rates than nations with low gun ownership. If anything it was the reverse, for reasons discussed below.

For example, though Norway has far and away the highest firearm ownership per capita in Western Europe, it nevertheless has the lowest murder rate. Other nations with high firearms ownership and comparably low murder rates include Denmark, Greece, Switzerland, Germany and Austria. Holland has a 50 percent higher murder rate despite having the lowest rate of firearm ownership in Europe. And Luxembourg, despite its total handgun ban, has a murder rate that is nine times higher than countries such as Norway and Austria.

Gun Control Laws Do Not Keep Criminals from Obtaining Guns

It turns out that in nations where guns are less available, criminals manage to get them anyway. After decades of ever-stricter gun controls, England banned handguns and confiscated them from all permit holders in 1997. Yet by 2000, England had the industrialized world's highest violent crime rate—twice that of the U.S. Despite the confiscation of law-abiding Englishmen's handguns, a 2002 report of England's National Crime Intelligence Service lamented that while "Britain has some of the strictest gun laws in the world, [i]t appears that anyone who wishes to obtain a firearm [illegally] will have little difficulty in doing so."

In the rare case in which gun bans work, murderers use other weapons. Eight decades of police-state enforcement of handgun prohibition have kept Russian gun ownership low, resulting in few gun murders. Yet Russia's murder rates have long been four times higher than those in the U.S. and 20 times higher than rates in countries such as Norway. Former Soviet nations like Lithuania also ban handguns and severely restrict other guns, yet have 10–15 times higher murder rates than European nations with much higher gun ownership.

Guns Keep Americans Safe

The very reason people desperately want to protect the right to keep and bear arms is so they can continue to defend and protect themselves—and others. Can you picture how many lives would have been saved [at Virginia Tech] if a faculty member or administrator or even a janitor who is licensed to carry a gun would have been able to take the killer out?

Mike Gallagher, "Preventing Another Massacre," Townhall.com, April 20, 2007. http://mikegallagher.townhall.com/columnists/MikeGallagher/2007/04/20/preventing_another_massacre.

More Guns Does Not Mean More Murder

Nor does the "more guns means more murder" belief square with our own experience. The earliest American figures, dating from just after World War II, showed both gun ownership and murder rates holding at low levels. Today our murder rates are almost identical, despite six decades of massive gun buying whereby Americans have come to own five times more guns than they did in 1946. The intervening years saw a dramatic increase in murder followed by a dramatic decrease. These trends had no relationship to gun ownership, which steadily rose all the while (especially handgun ownership).

American demographic data also refute the myth that fewer guns in a community mean less murder. The murder rate among African-Americans is six times higher than among whites. Does this mean African-Americans have more guns? No, ordinary law abiding African-Americans are markedly less likely than whites to own guns. But the argument for banning guns to everyone is refuted, since fewer guns for law abiding African-Americans does not mean fewer guns for African-American criminals. Incidentally, rural African-Americans own guns as frequently as whites, but the murder rate among them is only a tiny fraction of the urban African-American rate.

Regardless of race, the distinction between good people and criminals is vital. It is utterly false that most murderers are ordinary people who went wrong because they had guns. Almost all murderers have life histories of violence, restraining orders, substance abuse problems and/or a form of psychopathology. It's generally illegal for these people to have guns, but unlike good people, they ignore gun laws—just as they ignore laws against violence.

History Shows That Guns Keep Americans Safe

The "more guns means more murders" mythology also flies in the face of history. From the 1600s, American colonial law required that every household have a gun and that every military-age male be armed for militia service. Men too poor to buy guns were supplied with them by colonial governments and had to repay the cost in installments. To assure that every home and man was armed, officers periodically searched homes and men were required to muster with their guns. Despite this universal armament, murder was rare and few murders involved firearms.

Murder rates increased after the 1840s, by which time these armament requirements were no longer enforced and per capita gun ownership had become much lower. From the 1860s on, gun ownership increased sharply. Millions of men came home from the Civil War with their weapons; and firearms were even more widely distributed in the era of cheap pot metal guns (the "two dollar pistol") that followed. But this vast increase in guns—much deadlier guns than ever before—from the 1860s onward was accompanied by a substantially decreasing murder rate.

A few 19th century American states adopted gun controls because they had (and still have) severe violent crime rates. In most states, murders were few despite high gun ownership and virtually no gun control. Likewise, Europe had low murder rates prior to World War I despite high gun ownership and virtually no controls. Severe European gun laws appeared (for political reasons) in the tumultuous post–World War I era. Despite ever-stricter gun laws, both political and apolitical violence has increased apace in Europe.

Whether guns prevent or encourage crime and murder has been debated throughout America's history.

More Guns Does Not Mean More Crime

An increase in handgun ownership since 1966 has not resulted in an increase in handgun-related homicides or suicides.

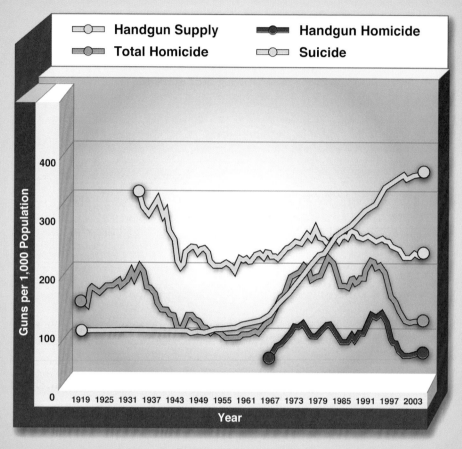

Taken from: www.guncite.com.

Guns Prevent Murder in Europe

If anything, a review of the European experience demonstrates more guns correlating with less murder. Nine European nations (including Germany, Austria, Denmark and Norway) have more than 15,000 guns per 100,000 members of the population. Nine others (including Luxembourg, Russia, and Hungary) have fewer than 5,000 guns per 100,000 members of the population. But the aggregate murder rates of these nine low-gun-ownership nations are three times higher than those of the nine high-gun-ownership nations.

Some groups, particularly the gun lobby, might argue that this shows how widespread gun ownership actually reduces violence rates. There is substantial evidence that this is true in the United States, where gun ownership for self-defense is very common. But there is no evidence that Norwegians, Germans and other Europeans often keep guns for defense.

The reason that European nations with more guns tend to have lower violence is political rather than criminological. Gun ownership generally has no effect on how much violent crime a society has. Violent crime is determined by fundamental economic and sociocultural factors, not the mere availability of just one of an innumerable bevy of potential murder instruments. Politicians

Anti-gun control advocates, like the Second Amendment Sisters, argue that widespread gun ownership reduces violence rates.

in nations with severe crime problems often think that banning guns will be a quick fix. But gun bans don't work; if anything, they make things worse. They disarm the law-abiding while being ignored by the violent and the criminal. Yet nations with severe violence problems tend to have severe gun laws. By the same token, the murder rates in handgun-banning U.S. cities—New York, Chicago, Washington, D.C.—are far higher than in states like Pennsylvania and Connecticut, where handguns are legal and widely owned.

Disarming Americans Helps Criminals

In sum, banning guns to the general public increases people's vulnerability and fails to reduce violence because the law-abiding citizenry are victims of violent crime, not perpetrators. Banning guns to felons, violent misdemeanants, juveniles and the insane (which our laws already do) is a good idea in general, though such laws are very difficult to enforce. Disarming those who only want to defend themselves, however, is a surefire road to empowering criminals at the expense of the innocent.

Analyze the essay:

1. What role does cause-effect reasoning play in this essay by Kates and Hehmeyer? List at least two examples.
2. The authors claim that people who own guns are usually not criminals, and thus their possession of guns does not threaten the safety of others. Do you agree with this claim? Why or why not? Explain your reasoning.

Guns Endanger Americans

Juliet A. Leftwich

In the following essay Juliet A. Leftwich argues that gun ownership should be restricted because guns cause the deaths of tens of thousands of Americans each year. She reprimands American lawmakers for failing to respond to tragic shootings with increased gun control laws. Leftwich suggests that many restrictions on gun ownership could be made without infringing on a person's right to bear arms. These include requiring background checks for all gun purchases, requiring registration and licensing, preventing criminals and the mentally ill from acquiring guns, and limiting the number of guns an individual can buy at a time. In the author's opinion, each of these is a reasonable restriction that could save the lives of thirty thousand Americans each year.

Leftwich is senior counsel of Legal Community Against Violence, a national law center formed in the wake of the 101 California St. assault weapon massacre in San Francisco in 1993.

Consider the following questions:

1. How did the United States and Scotland react differently to tragic school shootings, as described by the author?
2. How many people are killed per day by guns in the United States, as reported by Leftwich?
3. Name five ways in which the United States could reasonably restrict gun ownership, in the author's opinion.

Juliet A. Leftwich, "Worse than Iraq: Guns kill more Americans at home in six weeks than in four years of war," *The Recorder*, October 12, 2007. Copyright © 2007 ALM Media, Inc. Reproduced by permission.

On March 13, 1996, a former scoutmaster named Thomas Hamilton used four legally purchased handguns to slaughter 16 children and a teacher at an elementary school in Dunblane, Scotland. In response to the shooting, Great Britain banned virtually all handguns.

Three years later, on April 20, 1999, Columbine High School students Eric Harris and Dylan Klebold went on a shooting rampage in Colorado, killing 12 of their classmates and a teacher before ending their own lives. The federal government's response to the Columbine massacre? None, despite the fact that six other school shootings had taken place in America in the preceding 19 months.

America's Failure to Respond to Tragedy

Nearly eight years to the day after Columbine, on April 16, 2007, college student Seung-Hui Cho shot and killed 32 people at Virginia Tech before killing himself. That mass shooting—the worst in modern U.S. history—came only six months after five young girls were gunned down at an Amish schoolhouse in Pennsylvania. Was the federal government finally prompted to take action to prevent similar tragedies from happening in the future? Hardly.

In fact, the first statement from the White House after the Virginia Tech shooting was that President Bush supported the "right to bear arms." Later, he expressed condolences to the grieving families, but said that "now's not the time" to discuss any specific federal response to the tragedy. This sentiment was echoed by several members of Congress, including leading Democrats.

Perhaps it should come as no surprise, then, that with the six-month anniversary of the Virginia Tech shootings approaching next week, Congress still hasn't passed any new gun laws.

Guns Kill People—Lots of People.

How much more blood must be spilled before Congress decides that the time has come to take action? Guns are used to kill nearly 30,000 people each year in this country in homicides, suicides and unintentional shootings. Although most gun deaths receive little media attention, on average 32 people are killed in gun homicides each day in America—that's the equivalent of a daily Virginia Tech shooting. . . .

The United States has the weakest gun laws of all of the industrialized nations in the world (and, not surprisingly, the highest rate of firearm-related deaths). Congress could take many concrete steps short of a handgun ban to significantly reduce our nation's epidemic of gun violence.

Mourners at Virginia Tech attend a candlelight vigil for the victims of the shooting. Congress has not responded to the tragedy with any new gun laws.

Reasonable Restrictions on Gun Ownership

First and foremost, Congress could close the private sale loophole and require background checks on all prospective gun purchasers. Under current federal law, only federally licensed firearms dealers are required to perform background checks. Private sales, however, account for approximately 40 percent of all gun sales. As a result, except in the handful of states (like California) that have moved to close this loophole, criminals, young people and the mentally ill are easily able to buy guns from private sellers at gun shows and other locations nationwide.

Congress could also require registration of guns and licensing of gun owners, similar to the way our laws require registration of cars and licensing of drivers. Currently, the federal government has no idea who owns firearms in this country (indeed, thanks to the NRA [National Rifle Association], federal law actually prohibits the use of background check records to create any system of registration of firearms or firearms owners).

Registration laws are critical, however, because they allow law enforcement to quickly trace crime guns back to the individuals who purchased them, and to return lost or stolen firearms to their lawful owners. When registration laws require annual renewal and additional background checks, they also help ensure that gun owners remain eligible to possess firearms and do not illegally transfer their guns to others. Strong licensing laws are essential because they require gun owners to demonstrate their familiarity with existing gun laws and their ability to handle and store firearms safely. Registration and licensing laws are the cornerstone of responsible gun policy in industrialized nations worldwide.

Guns Endanger Americans

The number of U.S. civilians killed annually by guns is ten times the number of people killed in the September 11 terrorist attacks. More U.S. civilians are killed by guns every two years than the total number of U.S. soldiers killed in the entire eleven-year Vietnam War. . . . A child in the United States is far more likely to catch a bullet than the measles.

Bill Durston, "It's the Guns," *Sacramento News and Review*, April 26, 2007.

Guns Kill Thousands of Children Each Year

In 2004 nearly 3,000 children were killed in homicides, suicides, and accidents involving guns.

WA 49
OR 21
ID 16
MT 12
ND 10
MN 39
WI 43
MI 104
VT 3
ME 10
NH 4
MA 32
NY 89
PA 132
RI 4
CT 11
NV 27
UT 15
CO 48
WY 8
NE 15
IA 16
IL 143
IN 56
OH 80
WV 12
VA 76
NJ 48
CA 468
AZ 76
NM 28
KS 26
MO 61
KY 40
NC 70
MD 71
DE 9
OK 29
AR 16
TN 73
SC 44
TX 236
LA 88
MS 43
AL 52
GA 89
FL 111
AK 22
HI 0

*Total firearm deaths and homicide firearm deaths exclude firearm deaths by legal (police or corrections) intervention.

Taken from: U.S. Department of Health and Human Services, National Center for Health Statistics; National Center for Injury Prevention and Control; Children's Defense Fund.

Small Limitation That Could Save Lives

In addition, Congress could provide financial incentives to the states to submit all of their criminal and mental health records to the National Instant Criminal Background Check System (NICS). Currently, many prohibited persons are able to pass background checks because state records—including more than 90 percent of disqualifying mental health records and 25 percent of criminal convictions—have not been entered in NICS. (The House passed a long-languishing bill

A man waits at a gun shop for his gun registration check after making a purchase. Advocates say gun registration laws are critical because they allow police to trace guns used in crimes.

to provide such financial incentives last spring, but only after the NRA added last-minute amendments to compromise the legislation. That bill has stalled in the Senate.)

Moreover, Congress could:

- Authorize the Consumer Product Safety Commission to regulate firearms (the Consumer Product Safety Act currently exempts firearms and ammunition—and tobacco—from its requirements).

- Adopt a waiting period to give law enforcement adequate time to conduct background checks and allow gun purchasers an opportunity to "cool off."
- Limit the number of guns an individual may purchase at any one time (to prevent gun traffickers from buying large quantities of firearms and reselling them on the black market).
- Finally, Congress could undo the significant damage inflicted during the Bush administration by reinstating, and then strengthening, the assault weapon ban (which was allowed to expire in 2004 despite overwhelming public and law enforcement support), repealing the law granting the gun industry unprecedented immunity from most civil lawsuits (introduced by former NRA board member Sen. Larry Craig), repealing the so-called Tiahrt Amendment, which prohibits the Bureau of Alcohol, Tobacco, Firearms and Explosives from disclosing crime gun trace data (used to identify patterns of gun trafficking and released to the public until 2004), and repealing the law requiring firearm purchaser records to be destroyed after 24 hours. . . .

Guns Kill More People than the War in Iraq

When high-profile shootings like Columbine and Virginia Tech rock our nation, most Americans react with shock, horror and anguish. For some reason, however, those emotions have not yet translated into demands that our federal government actually do something to stop the carnage, despite the fact that opinion polls consistently show public support for stronger gun laws. Americans are outraged by the Iraq War and have begun to demand that the U.S. change its war policy. That outrage is completely justified: The Iraq War has taken the lives of more than 3,000 American soldiers.

But guns claim the lives of more than 3,000 people here at home every six weeks. Where's the outrage about that? The bloodbath at home will continue, day after day, year after year, unless and until the public demands that our federal legislators enact the common sense gun laws that we need.

Analyze the essay:

1. The author drives home her argument by likening the issue of gun control to the war in Iraq. What exactly is her argument, and does it cause you to agree or disagree with the position that America needs more gun control?

2. In this essay Leftwich focuses on how many Americans are killed each year by guns. In the previous essay authors Kates and Hehmeyer assert that lives are saved by guns. After reading both essays, with which author do you agree, and why?

Gun Ownership Causes Violence

Jonathon Gatehouse, Michael Friscolanti, and Luiza C.H. Savage

In the following essay Jonathon Gatehouse, Michael Friscolanti, and Luiza C.H. Savage argue that the widespread ownership of guns in America causes violence and murder. They lament the fact that shooting sprees have become so commonplace that they barely make the national news. Gatehouse, Friscolanti, and Savage argue that the government should protect Americans from needless gun violence by closing loopholes that put guns in the hands of people who use them to inflict violence on themselves or others. They refute the suggestion that more gun ownership protects Americans from violence: Nothing protects Americans from gun violence more than making guns harder to get, they conclude.

Gatehouse, Friscolanti, and Savage all work for *Maclean's*. Gatehouse is a national correspondent, Friscolanti is a senior writer, and Savage is *Maclean's* Washington bureau correspondent.

Consider the following questions:

1. List four incidents of gun violence the authors say received less attention than the 2007 Virginia Tech shootings.
2. What was the British government's reaction to the 1988 shooting in the town of Hungerford, as described by the authors?
3. What is, in the authors' opinion, a "national act of self-sabotage?"

Jonathon Gatehouse, Michael Friscolanti, and Luiza C.H. Savage, "In the Line of Fire," *Maclean's*, vol. 120, April 30, 2007, pp. 20–24. Copyright © 2007 by *Maclean's* magazine. Reproduced by permission.

Bright and early this past Easter Monday [in 2007] a 38-year-old accountant walked into a Troy, Mich., office with a pump-action shotgun, killed the 63-year-old receptionist and left two of his former bosses lying in pools of blood. The man had been fired on Thursday, and purchased the gun and ammunition on Good Friday. On March 27, a backyard poker game in Lake Worth, Fla., ended when one of the participants drew a gun instead of a straight, slaying three, and wounding four others. The evening before Valentine's Day, a trenchcoated 18-year-old opened fire in a Salt Lake City shopping mall, committing five random murders before turning the gun on himself. That very same night, a disgruntled Philadelphia investor burst into a board of directors meeting, killed three, wounded one, and took his own life.

The massacre of 32 staff and students, and wounding of 17 others at Virginia Tech, is an epic tragedy. (Among the dead was a former Montrealer, Jocelyne Couture-Nowak, who had been teaching French at the polytechnique for seven years, while her husband, Jerzy Nowak, taught agriculture.) But sadly, it's remarkable mostly for its scale—the worst shooting spree in American history—rather than its aberrance.

Shootings Are a Feature of American Life

The suspected gunman fits the profile all too well. Cho Seung-Hui, a 23-year-old senior who grew up in Korea but spent the past 14 years in the United States, had few friends, violent fantasies (his creative writing assignments were disturbing enough that course administrators referred him for counselling), and a fascination with weapons. Recent bad behaviour—reports of stalking and setting a dorm room on fire—weren't enough to spur authorizes into action. And without a felony conviction, there was nothing in federal or Virginia state laws to stop Cho, a permanent resident but not a citizen, from purchasing two handguns. Police say that they found the receipt for one, a 9-mm Glock, in his backpack.

Notes found in his room reportedly outlined his plans for revenge—the common theme among killers—on the "rich kids" and "deceitful chartatans" on campus, as well as linking him to two past bomb threats.

But similar, smaller acts of calculated violence are now an almost weekly feature of American life. So commonplace that they rarely make ripples beyond the communities where they occur. And in the case of impoverished victims and perpetrators, they go hardly noticed beyond the boundaries of their blighted neighbourhoods.

Tragedies That Go Unnoticed

"In the U.S., we have a couple of dozen mass killings every year," says James A. Fox, a professor of criminal justice at Northeastern University in Boston, and a noted authority on murder sprees. The intense media focus on events like the Virginia Tech shootings, last year's staying of five young

Local authorities investigate the schoolhouse where the shooting of five Amish girls occurred in Pennsylvania in October of 2006.

Handguns Are the Weapon of Choice for Murder

Handguns have consistently been used most often as the murder weapon in American homicides.

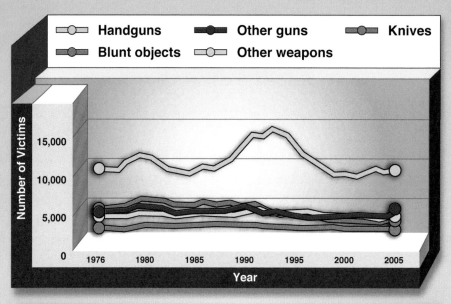

Year	Handgun	Other Gun	Knife	Blunt Object	Other Weapon
1976	8,651	3,328	3,343	912	2,546
1977	8,563	3,391	3,648	900	2,618
1978	8,879	3,569	3,685	937	2,490
1979	9,858	3,732	4,121	1,039	2,710
1980	10,552	3,834	4,439	1,153	3,061
1981	10,324	3,740	4,364	1,166	2,927
1982	9,137	3,501	4,383	1,032	2,957
1983	8,472	2,794	4,214	1,098	2,731
1984	8,183	2,835	3,956	1,090	2,626
1985	8,165	2,973	3,996	1,051	2,794
1986	9,054	3,162	4,235	1,176	3,018
1987	8,781	3,094	4,076	1,169	2,980
1988	9,375	3,162	3,978	1,296	2,869
1989	10,225	3,197	3,923	1,279	2,877
1990	11,677	3,395	4,077	1,254	3,037
1991	13,101	3,277	3,909	1,252	3,161
1992	13,158	3,043	3,447	1,088	3,024
1993	13,981	3,094	3,140	1,082	3,233
1994	13,496	2,840	2,960	963	3,071
1995	12,050	2,679	2,731	981	3,169
1996	10,731	2,533	2,691	917	2,777
1997	9,705	2,631	2,363	833	2,678
1998	8,844	2,168	2,257	896	2,805
1999	7,943	2,174	2,042	902	2,461
2000	7,985	2,218	2,099	727	2,556
2001	7,900	2,239	2,090	776	3,032
2002	8,286	2,538	2,018	773	2,588
2003	8,830	2,223	2,085	745	2,645
2004	8,304	2,357	2,133	759	2,595
2005	8,478	2,868	2,147	671	2,528

Taken from: Bureau of Justice Statistics, Homicide Trends in the U.S.: Weapons Used.
http://www.ojp.usdoj.gov/bjs/homicide/weapons.htm.

Amish girls at a rural Pennsylvania school, or the 1999 Columbine massacre, has created a perception that they are happening more frequently, but the number of such tragedies has stayed constant for close to 30 years. And while mass killings are an international phenomenon— the Dunblane massacre in Scotland, a rampage in Erfurt, Germany, that left 16 dead in 2002, and Canada's own École Polytechnique, Taber and Dawson College shootings among them—the U.S. remains their unquestioned epicentre. Fox ticks off his possible explanations: America's obsession with high-powered weapons, an

> ## Gun Ownership Causes Violence
>
> **When children kill children, we adults must do what we can to get the guns out of their hands.**
>
> Bruce Wellems, "Too Young to Die," *U.S. Catholic*, April 2004, p. 50.

"eclipse in community" and family breakdowns that have left more and more people isolated, and a popular culture that celebrates those who get even, and pities those who don't. "Most of these mass killers have a clear sense that they are right and other people are wrong," he says. "A clear sense that they are being victimized by an unfair system, and they go after the people they hold responsible."

What is also uniquely American is how its public and politicians are likely to respond to the latest in the lengthening line of gun tragedies—with real sorrow and outrage, but little or no action. Much of the country has grown used to buying its guns like milk and newspapers. Virginia, for example, ranks in the middle of the pack in terms of regulations. Potential purchasers do need background checks (unless they're shopping at a gun show), and you must be 18 to purchase an assault rifle—although mom or dad can give you one once you turn 12. And while it is illegal to bring any gun into educational institutions, including universities, it's easy to walk around with one off-campus. Police must issue a concealed weapons permit to anyone who asks.

Perhaps things are just less complicated abroad. After 16 people were shot dead by a lone gunman in the British town of Hungerford in 1988, the U.K. government reacted by tightening already strict gun control regulations and banning semi-automatic weapons. In the wake of the 1996 Dunblane killings, handguns were also banned. Both measures found widespread support. Australia's example is even more striking. Starting in the mid-1980s, 112 people were shot dead in 11 mass killings, culminating in an April 1996 massacre at the Port Arthur tourist site in Tasmania were yet another lone gunman took 35 lives and left 37 wounded. In response, Conservative Prime Minister John Howard introduced some of the world's toughest gun laws, banning almost all types of rifles and shotguns. The government then went even further, "buying back" and destroying some 700,000 such weapons already in private hands. (When problems began to surface with criminal gangs and handguns in 2000, pistols were also banned. Australia's firearm deaths have now tumbled from an annual average of 521 (including 93 homicides) prior to 1993 to 289 (56 homicides). Although violent crime was already on a downward trend, a recent University of Sydney study gives most of the credit to the gun control measures, noting that rate of decline in gun deaths has doubled. More to the point, there have been no mass shootings since the regulations took effect. . . .

Making Guns Harder to Get Helps Everyone

It's hard to escape the conclusion that America's patchwork of loopholes and exceptions, stretched and warped by the endless battle over citizens' constitutional "right" to bear arms, are at best ineffective, and at worst an act of national self-sabotage. According to the U.S. Department of Justice, there were 10,100 murders committed with firearms in 2005 . . . an average of 28 deaths a day (in Canada, that number was a mere 222, five times less per capita). Add in suicide and accidents, and the daily toll reaches 80. Every year, a further 200,000 people are lucky

enough to survive their brushes with firearms, although at an estimated health care cost of more than $100 billion. No one is even sure just how many guns there are in the United States. In 2004, the Harvard School of Public Health conducted a national telephone survey of 2,770 adults. Almost 40 per cent of households reported owning at least one firearm, with almost half of that group saying they had four or more. Extrapolated, the findings suggest there are at least 57 million private gun owners, with an estimated 283 million firearms—one for almost every American. . . .

[Cato Institute fellow Robert A.] Levy says [recent school] shootings show that gun bans are flawed as a matter of policy as well as law. "Virginia Tech is a perfect case in point—a guy is running around for two hours killing 32 people and no one can do anything about it. Why? Because no one is permitted to have a gun on the campus," said Levy. "It's nauseating, frankly, that no one can defend themselves in that kind of environment."

Queen Elizabeth lays a memorial wreath at Dunblane Primary School in Scotland where sixteen children and a teacher were slain by a gunman. The tragedy prompted the British government to ban handguns.

"That's absurd," [Ryerson University professor Wendy] Cukier says. The notion that gun crimes can be prevented by having more guns on the street is not supported by a shred of evidence, she says. "There is no question that these tragedies can occur anywhere regardless of the gun laws. There are no guarantees. But making it harder to get guns does more for public safety than making it easier."

Analyze the essay:

1. Jonathon Gatehouse, Michael Friscolanti, and Luiza C.H. Savage quote from several sources to support the points they make in their essay. Make a list of everyone they quote, including their credentials and the nature of their comments. Then, analyze the authors' sources: Are they credible? Are they well qualified to speak on this subject?

2. The authors of this essay argue that having more guns in the population leads to more violence because guns are used to kill people. The authors of the following essay argue that a greater number of guns leads to less violence because guns allow people to defend themselves against violence. After considering both positions, with which set of authors do you ultimately agree? Give examples of evidence that convinced you.

Gun Ownership Prevents Violence

John R. Lott Jr. and April L. Dabney

In the following essay John R. Lott Jr. and April L. Dabney argue that when law-abiding citizens are allowed to carry guns, they are in an excellent position to prevent violence. The authors say that although it might seem logical to assume that gun-free zones—areas in which guns are completely banned—would experience lower degrees of gun violence, in fact such areas are highly vulnerable to gun violence. They reason that if a violent person is going to commit a crime, that person is likely to target a gun-free zone to lessen the chance of confronting an armed person. For this reason, places in which people carry a gun for self-defense experience lower crime rates, claim the authors.

Lott is the author of *More Guns, Less Crime* and a resident scholar at the American Enterprise Institute, where Dabney is an assistant.

Consider the following questions:

1. What are right-to-carry laws, and how many states currently have them?
2. States that adopt right-to-carry laws experience what percent drop in violent attacks that result in murder, according to the authors?
3. What have annual surveys of crime victims by the U.S. Department of Justice determined about a person's level of safety when carrying a gun, according to Lott and Dabney?

Banning guns from the workplace seems like the obvious way to prevent workplace violence. At least that is the policy at ConocoPhillips and many other companies. The nation's largest oil refiner bans employees from storing locked guns in their cars while parked in company parking lots. The issue erupted this month when the NRA announced a boycott of Conoco and Phillips 66 gasoline stations and editorial pages across the country attacked the NRA's action as outrageous.

Gun-Free Zones Benefit Criminals

Two-and-a-half years ago, 12 employees at a Weyerhauser plant in Oklahoma were fired when they were caught unawares of a change in the company's ban on guns policy that was extended to the parking lot. The company had used trained dogs to find guns in employees' vehicles. Oklahoma's legislature overwhelmingly passed a law letting employees keep locked guns in their cars, but two firms, ConocoPhillips and the Williams Co., are challenging the law in court on the grounds that it endangers worker "safety."

Gun-free zones may appear like the solution to violence, but consider an analogy: Suppose a criminal is stalking you or your family. Would you feel safer putting a sign in front of your home saying, "This Home Is a Gun-Free Zone"? The answer seems pretty clear. Since law-abiding citizens will obey the signs, such "safe zones" simply mean that criminals have a lot less to worry about. Indeed, international data as well as data from across the United States indicate that criminals are much less likely to attack residents in their homes when they suspect that the residents own guns.

Gun Ownership Prevents Violence

A study funded by the Department of Justice . . . found that what felons fear most is not the police or the prison system, but their fellow citizens, who might be armed. One inmate told me, "When you gonna rob somebody you don't know, it makes it harder because you don't know what to expect out of them."

John Stossel, "Myths About Gun Control," RealClear Politics.com, October 19, 2005. www.realclearpolitics. com/Commentary/com-10_19_05_JS.html.

People Who Carry Guns Can Prevent Crime

Consider also the impact of right-to-carry laws—laws that automatically grant permits for concealed handguns once applicants pass a criminal background check, pay their fees and (when required) complete a training class. In 1985, just eight states had these laws. Today, 37 states do.

Examining all the multiple-victim public shootings from 1977 to 1999, one of the current authors with Bill Landes at the University of Chicago found that, on average, states that adopt right-to-carry laws experience a 60 percent drop in the rate at which the attacks occur and a 78 percent drop in the rate at which people are killed or injured from such attacks.

Some studies have shown that states that adopt right-to-carry gun laws experience as much as a 60 percent drop in the rate of gun-related attacks.

Firearms Are Not Used to Commit the Majority of Crimes

After 1996 less than 10 percent of nonfatal violent crimes (rape and sexual assault, robbery, and aggravated and simple assault) involved a firearm. Gun advocates argue this shows gun owners use their guns to prevent crime rather than cause it.

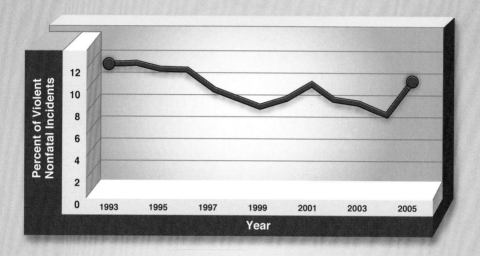

Nonfatal firearm incidents and victims, 1993–2005:

Year	Firearm Incidents	Firearm Victims	Firearm Crime Rate (victims per 1,000 residents)	Firearm Crimes as a Percent of All Violent Incidents
1993	1,054,820	1,248,250	5.9	11%
1994	1,060,800	1,286,860	6.0	11%
1995	902,680	1,050,900	4.9	10%
1996	845,220	989,930	4.6	10%
1997	680,900	795,560	3.6	9%
1998	557,200	670,480	3.0	8%
1999	457,150	562,870	2.5	7%
2000	428,670	533,470	2.4	7%
2001	467,880	524,030	2.3	9%
2002	353,880	430,930	1.9	7%
2003	366,840	449,150	1.9	7%
2004	280,890	331,630	1.4	6%
2005	419,640	477,040	2.0	9%

Taken from: National Crime Victimization Survey (NCVS), Bureau of Justice Statistics.

To the extent that such attacks still occurred in right-to-carry states, they overwhelmingly took place in so-called gun-free zones. The effect of right-to-carry laws is greater on multiple-victim public shootings than on other crimes, and for a simple reason: Increasing the probability that someone will be able to protect himself improves deterrence. Though it may be statistically unlikely that any person in particular in a crowd is carrying a concealed handgun, the probability that at least one person is armed is high.

For these attacks, the most important factor in determining the amount of harm is the length of time between the start of the attack and when someone with a gun can stop the attack. The longer the delay, the more people are harmed. By reducing the number harmed, right-to-carry laws take away much of the benefit these warped minds think they are achieving by their attack.

The vast majority of academic research finds that concealed handguns reduce violent crime, and, despite all the national studies that have been done, there is not a single refereed academic journal publication that claims a statistically significant increase in violent crime.

Gun Control Laws Cost Lives

The experiences in states with right-to-carry laws indicate that permit holders are extremely responsible and extremely law-abiding. Accidental gun deaths simply have not increased after states adopt these laws, and permit holders lose their permits for even the most trivial firearms-related violations at hundredths or thousandths of a percent. Police are important in deterring crime, but they almost always arrive after the crime has been committed. Annual surveys of crime victims in the United States by the Justice Department show that when confronted by a criminal, people are safest if they have a gun.

The real question is why the two firms bringing the case, ConocoPhillips and the Williams Co., are doing so. States supersede company decisions all the time on safety

Proponents of right-to-carry gun laws cite academic studies that show such laws reduce violent crime.

issues, and the legislature is clearly on record saying they believe that employees having access to their guns on net make them safer. The companies seem to have no more chance of winning this case than they do saying that they object to requirements that smoke alarms be installed. Given the NRA's belief that "The right-to-carry saves lives," it is hard to fault them for boycotting firms they think are endangering worker safety. Good intentions do not necessarily make good policy. What counts is whether the rules ultimately save lives.

The new rules that prohibit lawful gun-owners from having guns on company property look more likely to actually wind up costing more lives, rather than saving them.

Analyze the essay:

1. Lott and Dabney suggest that homes in gun-free areas essentially have a sign on their front lawn that reads, "This Home Is a Gun-Free Zone." In the authors' view this is an invitation for criminals to target people who are unable to defend themselves. What is your opinion of this argument? Do you believe that gun-free zones cause more crime to occur, or do you believe that gun-free zones keep people in those areas safer from gun violence? Explain your reasoning.

2. The authors of this essay (Lott and Dabney) and the authors of the previous essay (Gatehouse, Friscolanti, and Savage) use statistics to support their arguments. Yet they come to different conclusions on whether guns cause or prevent violence. List all the statistics used in each essay. Analyze their sources. After examining both sets of statistics, which do you find more persuasive? Why?

Gun Control Allows School Shootings to Occur

Roger D. McGrath

Roger D. McGrath argues in the following essay that school shootings could be prevented if more Americans were allowed to carry guns. He discusses several violent events in which law-abiding citizens were able to use their guns to chase off a criminal and prevent more people from being killed. Unfortunately, says McGrath, such heroes are rarely acknowledged by the public, and stories about lives saved by guns constitute a tiny percentage of all news reports. Furthermore, by prohibiting these people from carrying guns on their persons, restrictive gun control laws forced them to waste time running to their car to retrieve their weapon, thereby reducing the number of lives they could have saved. McGrath concludes that the best way to prevent school shootings and other violent crimes is to allow Americans to carry guns in self-defense.

McGrath, a retired history professor, is the author of *Gunfighters, Highwaymen, and Vigilantes*.

Consider the following questions:

1. What stories about guns rarely make the news, according to McGrath?
2. How did James Strand prevent more people from being killed during a school shooting in Edinboro, Pennsylvania?
3. Who is Tracy Bridges, and why does the author wish he would have been present at the 2007 Virginia Tech shooting?

Roger D. McGrath, "Making Our Schools Safe: the Virginia Tech shooting rampage highlights the vulnerability of our schools to gun violence, but the answer to the problem is *not* more gun-control laws," *New American*, vol. 23, May 28, 2007, pp. 13–15. Copyright © 2007 American Opinion Publishing Incorporated. Reproduced by permission.

At about the same time Cho Seung-Hui was shooting to death 32 unarmed students on the campus of Virginia Tech in Blacksburg, Virginia, a different scenario was unfolding near Waynesburg, Kentucky. Venus Ramey had had equipment stolen from the barn on her tobacco farm before. When she saw her dog dash into the barn, she suspected something was amiss. Balancing on her walker, the 82-year-old woman drew her snub-nosed .38 as Curtis Parrish, a would be thief, emerged. The revolver had a salutary effect on Parrish, who suddenly announced that he was leaving immediately. He intended to jump into a waiting car with three of his accomplices, but Ramey yelled, "Oh, no you won't," and opened fire, flattening the car's tires.

Guns Help People Thwart Crime

"I didn't even think twice," she later said. "If they'd even dared come close to me, they'd be six feet under by now." While Ramey held the men at gunpoint, she flagged down a passing motorist, who then called 911. Sheriff's deputies eventually took the men into custody. Guns are used daily by private citizens like Ramey to thwart crime and apprehend criminals. Much of the time simply brandishing a firearm is enough to do the job. Even low estimates of such actions state that they occur tens of thousands of times a year. Gary Kleck, a Florida State University criminologist, argues that the figure is upwards of two million a year. Although guns are clearly used effectively by peaceable, law-abiding citizens far in excess of criminal misuse, such stories rarely make the news. Stories like Ramey's do nothing to further the disarmament agenda of the mainstream media. . . .

Americans Care Too Much About "Why"

I think about this while reading analysis after analysis of Korean immigrant Cho Seung-Hui. Was he alienated, autistic, sexually frustrated, drug addled, insane? Did he

An example of private citizens carrying guns to thwart crime is the tale of Venus Ramey, an eighty-two-year-old woman who confronted thieves on her property with a handgun.

play too many video games, watch too much television, view too many violent movies? This all seems less than relevant. There are a million and one reasons for criminal behavior. We, as a society, can't fix them all—although there are some that we might wish to work on. However, given the right arms and training, we can defend against such acts.

Instructive is what occurred in 2002 at another Virginia college. At Appalachian Law School in Grundy, Nigerian immigrant Peter Odighizuwa began a rampage, shooting to death a dean, a professor, and a student, and wounding three students. Upon hearing the gunfire, law students Tracy Bridges and Mikael Gross, independently, dashed to their cars to retrieve their own handguns. Bridges returned with a .357 magnum and Gross

A Time Line of Fatal School Shootings in the United States

February 2, 1996 Moses Lake, WA	Two students and one teacher are killed, one other wounded when fourteen-year-old Barry Loukaitis opened fire in his algebra class.
October 1, 1997 Pearl, MS	Two students killed and seven wounded by Luke Woodham, sixteen, who was also accused of killing his mother. He and his friends were said to be outcasts who worshipped Satan.
March 24, 1998 Jonesboro, AR	Four students and one teacher are killed, ten others wounded outside as Westside Middle School emptied during a false fire alarm. Mitchell Johnson, thirteen, and Andrew Golden, eleven, shot at their classmates and teachers from the woods.
May 21, 1998 Springfield, OR	Two students killed, twenty-two others wounded in the cafeteria at Thurston High School by fifteen-year-old Kip Kinkel. Kinkel had been arrested and released a day earlier for bringing a gun to school. His parents were later found dead at home.
April 20, 1999 Littleton, CO	Fourteen students (including killers) and one teacher killed, twenty-three others wounded at Columbine High School in the nation's deadliest school shooting. Eric Harris, eighteen, and Dylan Klebold, seventeen, had plotted for a year to kill at least five hundred and blow up their school. At the end of their hour-long rampage, they turned their guns on themselves.
November 19, 1999 Deming, NM	Victor Cordova Jr., twelve, shot and killed Araceli Tena, thirteen, in the lobby of Deming Middle School.
February 29, 2000 Mount Morris Township, MI	Six-year-old Kayla Rolland shot dead at Buell Elementary School near Flint, Michigan. The assailant was identified as a six-year-old boy with a .32-caliber handgun.
March 10, 2000 Savannah, GA	Two students killed by Darrell Ingram, nineteen, while leaving a dance sponsored by Beach High School.
March 5, 2001 Santee, CA	Two killed and thirteen wounded by Charles Andrew Williams, fifteen, firing from a bathroom at Santana High School.
April 14, 2003 New Orleans, LA	One fifteen-year-old killed, and three students wounded at John McDonogh High School by gunfire from four teenagers (none were students at the school). The motive was gang-related.
March 21, 2005 Red Lake, MN	Jeff Weise, sixteen, killed grandfather and companion, then arrived at school where he killed a teacher, a security guard, five students, and finally himself, leaving a total of ten dead.
August 24, 2006 Essex, VT	Christopher Williams, twenty-seven, looking for his ex-girlfriend at Essex Elementary School, shot two teachers, killing one and wounding another. Before going to the school, he had killed the ex-girlfriend's mother.
October 3, 2006 Nickel Mines, PA	Thirty-two-year-old Carl Charles Roberts IV entered the one-room West Nickel Mines Amish School and shot ten schoolgirls, ranging in age from six to thirteen years old, and then himself. Five of the girls and Roberts died.
April 16, 2007 Blacksburg, VA	A twenty-three-year-old Virginia Tech student, Cho Seung-Hui, killed two in a dorm, then killed thirty more two hours later in a classroom building. His suicide brought the death toll to thirty-three, making the shooting rampage the most deadly in United States history. Fifteen others were wounded.
February 8, 2008 Baton Rouge, LA	A nursing student shot and killed two women and then herself in a classroom at Louisiana Technical College in Baton Rouge.
February 14, 2008 DeKalb, IL	Gunman kills seven students and himself and wounds fifteen more when he opens fire on a classroom at Northern Illinois University. The gunman, Stephen P. Kazmierczak, was identified as a former graduate student at the university in 2007.

Taken from: InfoPlease, 2008.

a 9 millimeter to find Odighizuwa exiting from a campus building. From different angles both Bridges and Gross leveled their weapons at Odighizuwa. Bridges yelled to the killer, "Drop your gun!" Odighizuwa did so and several students then pinned him to the ground. End of rampage.

Odighizuwa's shooting spree was widely reported. It was also widely reported that he was subdued by Appalachian students. What went mostly unreported, however, was the fact that gun-toting students were responsible for Odighizuwa having a sudden change of attitude. John Lott, Jr., a well-published researcher and writer on gun issues, said that in a Lexis-Nexis search he found that only four of 208 stories mentioned that Bridges and Gross had guns. Other researchers had similar results. On the other hand, many of the stories did mention that Odighizuwa was distraught over failing grades and faced cultural differences. Psychoanalysis of the perpetrator was evidently more important than a clear narrative of events. Those interested in the former will have plenty of time to study Odighizuwa. To avoid the death penalty, he pleaded guilty to murder and is doing a life term in prison.

Some School Shooting Deaths Prevented with Guns

In Edinboro, Pennsylvania, 14-year-old Andrew Wurst came to a Parker Middle School graduation dance being held on the patio of a restaurant with a .25-caliber semi-automatic handgun. "We were all dancing and having a great time, and we heard a bang and everybody thought it was a balloon or firecracker," said a student. Science teacher John Gillette dropped to the ground dead with a bullet in his head. Wurst fired three more times, wounding another teacher and two students before the owner of the restaurant, James Strand, armed with a shotgun, put him to flight. Strand chased Wurst into a nearby field and convinced him to drop his gun and surrender. Wurst pleaded guilty to third-degree murder and was sentenced to 30–60 years in prison.

In 1997, 16-year-old Luke Woodham beat and stabbed to death his 50-year-old mother, then grabbed a .30-30 lever-action rifle and headed to his high school in Pearl, Mississippi. He shot to death his ex-girlfriend and a friend of hers and wounded seven other students. Upon hearing the first shots, Joel Myrick, the vice principal of Pearl High, ran to his pickup truck to get his .45. He had a concealed gun permit but was prohibited by law from carrying the gun onto school property. By the time Myrick caught up with Woodham, the student was hopping into his car with the intention of driving to nearby Pearl Junior High and continuing the shooting spree. Woodham started to pull away but suddenly saw Myrick aiming his gun. Unnerved, Woodham crashed the car. "Here was this monster killing kids in my school," said Myrick, "and the minute I put a gun to his head he was a kid again."

> ## Gun Control Causes School Shootings
>
> There was one thing this killer [at Red Lake High School, Minnesota] knew. He knew he would not face an armed teacher or principal while he slaughtered innocents. In addition, he had useless gun control laws and Liberals to thank for the fact his victims were helpless. More gun control laws will not only not prevent future mass murders they will, in fact, only assure more of them will happen.
>
> Doug Hagin, "How to Stop School Shootings?" Renew America.com, March 22, 2005. www.renewamerica.us/columns/hagin/050322.

Unsung Heroes

Woodham pleaded not guilty by reason of insanity and went to trial. The jury rejected his defense and found him guilty of murder. Woodham was sentenced to life in prison. One would assume that Myrick was universally hailed as a hero. Not so. During the summer of 1999, he took graduate courses in education at Harvard University. "Once people found out my story," said Myrick, "I got a lot of dirty looks and strange stares. A few people confronted me." He was treated very differently by *Soldier of Fortune* magazine. At the urging of Wayne Laugesen, a Colorado journalist and friend of Bob Brown, the publisher of *Soldier*

Sixteen-year-old Luke Woodham was sentenced to life in prison for the shooting deaths of his mother and classmates at Pearl High School in Mississippi in 1997.

of Fortune, the magazine awarded Myrick its Humanitarian Award of 1999 during its annual convention in Las Vegas in October.

Let Americans Defend Themselves

If Tracy Bridges, Mikael Gross, and Joel Myrick had been carrying their guns, instead of having to sprint to their cars in distant parking lots, more students might be alive today. By contrast, restaurant owner James Strand's rapid response may have saved several lives. The attempt to make school campuses "gun-free zones" has clearly backfired. Nowhere is that more evident than at Virginia Tech. In 2006, state legislators in Virginia considered a bill that would have allowed students and professors with concealed-carry permits to bring their guns onto college campuses. When the bill died in committee, Virginia Tech associate vice president Larry Hincker declared, "I'm sure the university community is appreciative of the General Assembly's actions because this will help parents, students, faculty and visitors feel safe on our campus." He later wrote in an editorial for the *Roanoke Times*, "Guns don't belong in classrooms. They never will. Virginia Tech has a very sound policy preventing same."

Cho Seung-Hui brought two guns onto the campus of Virginia Tech. He shot, reloaded, shot, walked from room to room, shot, reloaded. He was in no hurry. He had no expectation that a fellow student or a faculty member might shoot back. Virginia Tech is a gun-free zone. If only a Tracy Bridges had been there with his .357 magnum.

Analyze the essay:
1. Roger D. McGrath is a retired university professor. In your opinion, does this make him particularly qualified to write on the issue of school shootings? Why or why not?
2. In this essay the author suggests that people on school campuses should be allowed to carry guns so they can reduce the frequency and deadliness of school shootings. How do you think each of the other authors in this chapter might respond to this suggestion? List each speaker and write two or three sentences on what you think their response might be.

Gun Control Can Prevent School Shootings

Paul Helmke

In the following essay Paul Helmke argues that tighter gun laws can prevent school shootings. He states that America has an unacceptable rate of gun violence—about thirty-two people are killed each day by guns, a figure Helmke says is equivalent to one Virginia Tech massacre every single day. He suggests that America should protect its students by requiring background checks for gun purchases, limiting the number of guns allowed to be purchased by any one person, and banning the types of weapons used by the Virginia Tech and Northern Illinois University shooters. Helmke concludes that America's students deserve to go to school in peaceful places where they do not fear being gunned down as a result of lax gun laws.

Paul Helmke became president of the Brady Campaign/Center to Prevent Gun Violence in mid-July 2006.

Consider the following questions:

1. How many multiple murders occurred in the United States in the first half of February 2008, according to the author?
2. What effect might an assault weapons ban have on school shootings, in Helmke's opinion?
3. What events led to the creation of the National Firearms Act of 1934, as reported by Helmke?

Paul Helmke, "We Can Do Something About Gun Violence in America," *Huffington Post*, February 21, 2008. Reproduced by permission.

Our thoughts and prayers are with the victims and families touched by the recent gun violence at Northern Illinois University. At a time when the country confronts one mass shooting after another—six separate multiple murders across the country in just the first two weeks of February [2008]—the nation is faced with a critical choice:

Make It Harder for People to Get Guns

Do we give up and say we can't do anything about these tragedies? Or do we take common-sense steps today to make it harder for dangerous people to get dangerous weapons?

Every day in America, 32 people are murdered with guns. That's a daily Virginia Tech. This tragic figure is not due to natural or mysterious forces beyond our control. People cause this problem and people can fix it.

Proponents of gun control say that gun shows need to be more regulated because of unlicensed gun dealers who sell guns without a background check.

Over the years, the Brady Campaign has proposed numerous common-sense measures to reduce and prevent gun violence. It may be difficult to stop "suicide shooters" like the Northern Illinois University killer, but there are steps we can take as a nation.

Ways to Prevent School Shootings

We can require background checks for every gun transaction in America. Current federal law requires that only federally licensed gun dealers do a computer check on the criminal backgrounds of purchasers who buy guns from them. Yet there is no such restriction on unlicensed sellers who sell guns at gun shows, from the trunk of their cars or at their kitchen tables. If we want to make it harder for dangerous people to get dangerous weapons, we must close this loophole, and require that all gun buyers undergo a background check.

> ## Gun Control Can Prevent School Shootings
>
> **Educational and law enforcement professionals agree that a policy tightly restricting or banning firearms on campus should be an essential part of every school security plan.**
>
> Brady Center to Prevent Gun Violence, "No Gun Left Behind: The Gun Lobby's Campaign to Push Guns into Colleges and Schools," May 2007. www.bradycenter.org/xshare/pdf/reports/no-gun-left-behind.pdf.

We can limit bulk purchases of handguns to cut down on the illegal gun trade. Gun buyers currently have no federal limits on the number of guns they can buy at one time. Gun traffickers take advantage of the unlimited number of guns they can purchase at a time in order to sell guns to criminals and gangs. Combine this weakness in the law with the use of "straw purchasers" or with unlicensed sellers, and a gun trafficker can buy dozens of cheap handguns at a time and re-sell them on the street at a hefty markup. Who personally needs more than 12 or even 24 handguns per year? We should limit bulk purchases of handguns to cut down on gun trafficking and the supply of weapons to the illegal market.

We can also ban the sale of military-style assault weapons and high capacity ammunition magazines. One thing the Virginia Tech and Northern Illinois University

Proponents for gun control argue that a ban on assault weapons will keep local law enforcement agencies from being outgunned by criminals.

shooters had in common was that they both used high capacity ammunition magazines that would have been prohibited under the Federal Assault Weapons Ban that expired in 2004. Furthermore, there is no reason that weapons of war should be made easily available to citizens who are not police officers or in the military. We should support our local law enforcement officers as they put their lives on the line to protect ours, and reduce the chances that they will be out-gunned on our streets by these high-powered firearms.

Gun Laws Are "Tragically Weak"

The Northern Illinois University shooting happened on the anniversary of Chicago's "St. Valentine's Day Massacre," February 14, 1929, and a day before the anniversary of the attempted assassination of President-elect Franklin D. Roosevelt, and the killing of Chicago Mayor Anton Cermak on February 15, 1933. Those events led to one of the few gun control laws still on the books, the National Firearms Act of 1934. Our recent gun violence should also lead us to take action.

As we grieve with the victims and families of this latest mass shooting, I call on college and university presidents across America to join with us in demanding that candidates for president, the U.S. Congress, and state legislatures across the country support meaningful action to prevent gun violence, such as the measures listed above.

Our gun laws today are tragically weak. Much more could be done to help make our schools and communities safer.

Analyze the essay:

1. Paul Helmke uses history, facts, and examples to make his argument that gun control can prevent school shootings. He does not, however, use any quotations to support his point. If you were to rewrite this article and insert quotations, what authorities might you quote from? Where would you place these quotations to bolster the points Helmke makes?

2. In this section, six authors have made different arguments about gun control in America. Make a list of the argument in each essay that most struck you. Then, choose the most compelling argument presented in the section, and explain why you support it.

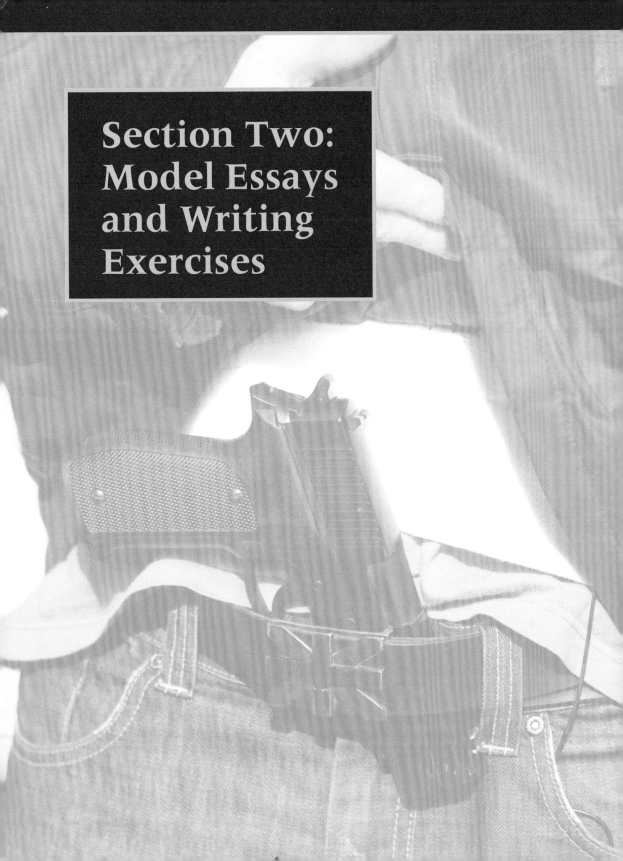

Section Two:
Model Essays
and Writing
Exercises

The Five-Paragraph Essay

An *essay* is a short piece of writing that discusses or analyzes one topic. The five-paragraph essay is a form commonly used in school assignments and tests. Every five-paragraph essay begins with an *introduction*, ends with a *conclusion*, and features three *supporting paragraphs* in the middle.

The Thesis Statement. The introduction includes the essay's thesis statement. The thesis statement presents the argument or point the author is trying to make about the topic. The essays in this book all have different thesis statements because they are making different arguments about gun control.

The thesis statement should clearly tell the reader what the essay will be about. A focused thesis statement helps determine what will be in the essay; the subsequent paragraphs are spent developing and supporting its argument.

The Introduction. In addition to presenting the thesis statement, a well-written introductory paragraph captures the attention of the reader and explains why the topic being explored is important. It may provide the reader with background information on the subject matter or feature an anecdote that illustrates a point relevant to the topic. It could also present startling information that clarifies the point of the essay or put forth a contradictory position that the essay will refute. Further techniques for writing an introduction are found later in this section.

The Supporting Paragraphs. The introduction is then followed by three (or more) supporting paragraphs. These are the main body of the essay. Each paragraph presents and develops a *subtopic* that supports the essay's thesis statement. Each subtopic is spearheaded by a *topic sentence* and supported by its own facts, details, and examples. The writer can use various kinds of supporting material and details to back up the topic of each supporting paragraph. These may include statistics, quotations from people with special knowledge or expertise, historic facts, and anecdotes. A rule of writing is that specific and concrete examples are more convincing than vague, general, or unsupported assertions.

The Conclusion. The conclusion is the paragraph that closes the essay. Its function is to summarize or reiterate the main idea of the essay. It may recall an idea from the introduction or briefly examine the larger implications of the thesis. Because the conclusion is also the last chance a writer has to make an impression on the reader, it is important that it not simply repeat what has been presented elsewhere in the essay but close it in a clear, final, and memorable way.

Although the order of the essay's component paragraphs is important, they do not have to be written in the order presented here. Some writers like to decide on a thesis and write the introduction paragraph first. Other writers like to focus first on the body of the essay and write the introduction and conclusion later.

Pitfalls to Avoid

When writing essays about controversial issues such as gun control, it is important to remember that disputes over the material are common precisely because there are many different perspectives. Remember to state your arguments in careful and measured terms. Evaluate your topic fairly—avoid overstating negative qualities of one perspective or understating positive qualities of another. Use examples, facts, and details to support any assertions you make.

The Cause-and-Effect Essay

The previous section of this book provided you with samples of published persuasive writing on gun control. All were persuasive, or opinion, essays making certain arguments about gun control. They were also either *cause-and-effect* essays or used cause-and-effect reasoning. This section will focus on writing your own cause-and-effect essay.

Cause and effect is a common method of organizing and explaining ideas and events. Simply put, cause and effect is a relationship between two things in which one thing makes something else happen. The *cause* is the reason why something happens. The *effect* is what happens as a result.

A simple example would be a car not starting because it is out of gas. The lack of gas is the cause; the failure to start is the effect. Another example of cause-and-effect reasoning is found in Viewpoint Two. Author Juliet A. Leftwich describes how guns cause the deaths of nearly thirty thousand Americans every year.

Not all cause-and-effect relationships are as clear-cut as these two examples. It can be difficult to determine the cause of an effect, especially when talking about society-wide causes and effects. For example, smoking and cancer have been long associated with each other, but not all cancer patients smoked, and not all smokers get cancer. It took decades of debate and research before the U.S. surgeon general concluded in 1964 that smoking cigarettes causes cancer (and even then, that conclusion was disputed by tobacco companies for many years thereafter). Similarly, in Viewpoint One, authors Don B. Kates and Carol Hehmeyer suggest that guns are *not* the cause of murder in America. They argue that criminals are the cause of murder, and guns are most often used by law-abiding citizens to thwart crime and murder. As this example shows, creating and evaluating cause and effect involves both collecting convincing evidence and exercising critical thinking.

Types of Cause-and-Effect Essays

In general, there are three types of cause-and-effect essays. In one type, many causes can contribute to a single effect. Supporting paragraphs would each examine one specific cause. For example, Jonathon Gatehouse, Michael Friscolanti, and Luiza C.H. Savage in Viewpoint Three argue that several factors contribute to the problem of gun violence in America. The availability of guns, gun loopholes and exceptions, and the problem of stolen guns are the causes; together they have resulted in the deaths of tens of thousands of people—the effect.

Another type of cause-and-effect essay examines multiple effects from a single cause. The thesis posits that one event or circumstance has multiple results. An example from this volume is found in Viewpoint Four by John R. Lott Jr. and April L. Dabney. Lott and Dabney argue that a single cause—gun control—can have multiple effects on Americans, including restricting their ability to defend themselves from criminals; violating their Second Amendment rights; and increasing the murder rate. Gun control is the single cause; safety and rights issues are the multiple effects.

A final type of cause-and-effect essay is one that examines a series of causes and effects—a "chain of events" in which each link is both the effect of what happened before and the cause of what happens next. Model Essay Three later in this section of this book provides one example. The author describes the story of Seung-Hui Cho, who killed thirty-two people at Virginia Polytechnic Institute and State University (Virginia Tech) in 2007. Social and emotional developmental problems as a child caused Cho to become a deeply isolated, disturbed person. He developed severe mental health problems that were not caught by Virginia Tech administrators or by the gun dealers who sold him his weapons. These are just a few events in a chain that led him to commit the worst mass shooting in American history, and an example of a chain-of-events sequence in which an initial cause can have successive repercussions down the line.

Tips to Remember

In writing argumentative essays about controversial issues such as gun control, it is important to remember that disputes over cause-and-effect relationships are part of the controversy. Gun control and its related issues are complex matters that have multiple effects and multiple causes, and often there is disagreement over what causes what. One needs to be careful and measured in how arguments are expressed. Avoid overstating cause-and-effect relationships if they are unwarranted.

Another pitfall to avoid in writing cause-and-effect essays is to mistake chronology for causation. Just because event X came before event Y does not necessarily mean that X caused Y. Additional evidence may be needed, such as documented studies or similar testimony from many people. Likewise, correlation does not necessarily imply causation. Just because two events happened at the same time does not necessarily mean they are causally related. Again, additional evidence is needed to verify the cause/effect argument.

In this section, you will read some model essays on gun control that use cause-and-effect arguments and do exercises that will help you write your own.

Words and Phrases Common in Cause-and-Effect Essays

accordingly	it then follows that
as a result of	since
because	so
consequently	so that
due to	subsequently
for	therefore
for this reason	this is how
if . . . then	thus

The Causes of Gun Violence in America

Editor's Notes The first model essay examines multiple causes of gun violence. The author argues that availability of guns, lax background checks, and the problem of stolen guns contribute to high rates of gun-related death and injury. The essay is structured as a five-paragraph essay in which each paragraph contributes a supporting piece of evidence to develop the argument.

The notes in the margin point out key features of the essay and will help you understand how the essay is organized. Also note that all sources are cited using Modern Language Association (MLA) style.* For more information on how to cite your sources see Appendix C. In addition, consider the following:

1. How does the introduction engage the reader's attention?
2. What cause-and-effect techniques are used in the essay?
3. What purpose do the essay's quotes serve?
4. Does the essay convince you of its point?

■ Refers to thesis and topic sentences

■ Refers to supporting details

Paragraph 1

The United States has one of the highest rates of gun violence in the entire industrialized world. Each day, dozens of people of are killed in gun-related homicides, accidents, and suicides. Why is the problem of gun violence in America so severe? An examination of the underlying causes of gun violence exposes three main causes of the problem—the widespread availability of guns in our

This is the essay's thesis statement. It tells the reader what will be argued in the following paragraphs.

* Editor's Note: In applying MLA style guidelines in this book, the following simplifications have been made: Parenthetical text citations are confined to direct quotations only; electronic source documentation in the Works Cited list omits date of access, page ranges, and some detailed facts of publication.

culture; the insufficiency of background checks; and the problem of stolen guns. Each of these problems puts guns in the hands of the wrong people, resulting in the death of loved one after loved one.

Paragraph 2

The primary cause of gun violence in America is found right in the problem's name: guns. The sheer number and availability of guns in the United States has helped build a culture in which shootings are so commonplace, small ones are routinely ignored by the national news. As authors Jonathon Gatehouse, Michael Friscolanti, and Luiza C.H. Savage have noticed, "Acts of calculated violence are now an almost weekly feature of American life. So commonplace that they rarely make ripples beyond the communities where they occur"(20). Gatehouse, Friscolanti, and Savage estimate that at least 57 million Americans own about 283 million guns—that is one gun for almost every American. It is no wonder, then, that guns are used as the weapon of choice in homicides, suicides, and accidental shootings, resulting in the deaths of nearly thirty thousand people every year.

Paragraph 3

Another cause of gun violence in America is that insufficient background checks are performed on potential gun buyers. Under federal law, the only firearms dealers who are required to perform background checks on gun buyers are federally licensed ones. Those who sell guns privately and at gun shows—even if the sale is legal—are not required to check if the person they are selling a gun to is underage, has a criminal past, or has a history of mental illness. According to some estimates, such sales make up 40 percent of all gun sales! Lax background check systems have had disastrous consequences for the victims of irresponsible gun owners. Indeed, Seung-Hui Cho, who killed thirty-two people at Virginia Tech in the worst shooting in American history, was able to legally buy a gun despite the fact that he had a history of mental

This quote was taken from Viewpoint Three. When you see particularly striking quotes, save them to use to support points in your essays.

This fact from Viewpoint Two helps support the paragraph's main idea: that the availability of guns causes violence. Get in the habit of supporting points you make with facts, quotes, and anecdotes.

This is the topic sentence of Paragraph 3. It is a subset of the essay's thesis. It tells what specific point this paragraph will make.

This fact was taken from Viewpoint Two in this book. Look for other pieces of information that can be used to support the points you make in your essays.

illness. Insufficient background checks failed to identify him as a person who should not be trusted with a gun. For this reason, background checks are part of what one author has called "the cornerstone of responsible gun policy in industrialized nations worldwide," and should be a part of gun control practiced in the United States (Leftwich).

<aside>
"Indeed" and "For this reason" are transitional phrases that keep the ideas flowing. See Preface B for a list of words and phrases commonly found in cause-and-effect essays.
</aside>

Paragraph 4

A third—but surely not final—cause of gun violence in the United States is the problem of stolen guns. According to the FBI, nearly 1.7 million guns were reported stolen between 1995 and 2005, and only 40 percent of those were recovered. More than 80 percent of these guns are taken from homes or cars. Even if the owners of these guns bought them legally and planned to use them responsibly, once in the hands of criminals they are likely to be used for violence, crime, and even murder.

<aside>
This is the topic sentence of Paragraph 4. It tells what idea this paragraph will focus on.
</aside>

<aside>
This fact was taken from Appendix A in this book. This book contains many valuable resources for writing an essay on gun control.
</aside>

Paragraph 5

The availability of guns, the insufficiency of background checks, and the problem of stolen guns are just a few factors contributing to the problem of gun violence in America. Over the years, they have caused the deaths of hundreds of thousands of people and left countless others physically injured and emotionally scarred. Isn't it time we got our nation's guns under control?

<aside>
Note how the author wraps up the essay's main points in a clear and memorable way.
</aside>

Works Cited

Gatehouse, Jonathon, Michael Friscolanti, and Luiza C.H. Savage. "In the Line of Fire." *Maclean's* 30 Apr. 2007.

Leftwich, Juliet A. "Worse than Iraq: Guns Kill More Americans at Home in Six Weeks than in Four Years of War." *Recorder* 12 Oct. 2007.

Exercise 1A: Create an Outline from an Existing Essay

It often helps to create an outline of the five-paragraph essay before you write it. The outline can help you organize the information, arguments, and evidence you have gathered during your research.

For this exercise, create an outline that could have been used to write *The Causes of Gun Violence in America*. This "reverse engineering" exercise is meant to help familiarize you with how outlines can help classify and arrange information.

To do this you will need to

1. articulate the essay's thesis,
2. pinpoint important pieces of evidence,
3. flag quotes that supported the essay's ideas, and
4. identify key points that supported the argument.

Part of the outline has already been started to give you an idea of the assignment.

Outline

I. Paragraph One
Write the essay's thesis:

II. Paragraph Two
Topic: The availability of guns in the United States

Supporting Detail i. There are at least 57 million Americans who own about 283 million guns—that is one gun for almost every American.

Supporting Detail ii.

III. Paragraph Three
Topic:

i. Those who sell guns privately and at gun shows—even if the sale is legal—are not required to check if the person they are selling a gun to is underage, has a criminal past, or has a history of mental illness.

ii.

IV. Paragraph Four

Topic: How stolen guns contribute to gun violence in America

    i.

    ii.

V. Paragraph Five

    i. Write the essay's conclusion:

The Consequences of Gun Control

Editor's Notes The second model essay embodies a different form of cause-and-effect essay: multiple effects from a single cause. The thesis suggests that one event or circumstance has multiple results. In the case of this essay, the author argues that increasing gun control has multiple negative effects on society. In clear, distinct paragraphs the author outlines three different effects that gun control has on society, and she supports her points with facts, anecdotes, and quotes.

As you did for the first model essay, take note of the essay's components and how they are organized. (The sidebars in the margins will help you identify the essay's pieces and their purpose.)

Paragraph 1

After every school and workplace shooting, Americans ask each other in anguish, "How could this tragedy have been prevented?" Some believe the answer lies in laws that tighten restrictions on gun ownership, or what are called gun control laws. Such laws make it more difficult to buy a gun, for example, or limit the places to which private gun owners may bring their guns. But gun control is not the answer to America's problems—indeed, it may actually be its cause. **Gun control has negative effects on society and, therefore, should be resisted at all costs.**

This is the essay's thesis statement. It gets to the heart of the author's argument.

Paragraph 2

Contrary to popular opinion, guns are primarily used to *prevent* crime and murder, not perpetrate it. In this way, banning or restricting private gun ownership increases crime and murder. Using data from 1977 to 1999, researchers at the University of Chicago found that states

What is the topic sentence of Paragraph 2? (Hint: It is not the first sentence.)

in which citizens are allowed to carry their guns in public experienced a 60 percent drop in criminal attacks and a 78 percent drop in murders and injuries that result from these attacks. In other words, because they were armed, private citizens were able to thwart a criminal's plans to commit crime. Therefore, when you reduce citizens' right to own and carry guns, you increase criminals' ability to terrorize, murder, and steal. This is precisely why nations like Norway, Denmark, Greece, Switzerland, Germany, and Austria—nations with high gun ownership rates—experience lower murder rates than nations in which gun ownership is much lower.

This is a *supporting detail*. It directly supports the topic sentence, helping to prove it true.

From which viewpoint in Section I was this information taken?

Paragraph 3

A second negative effect of gun control is that it robs Americans of their right to defend themselves. In fact, gun control is so harmful to Americans that it should be viewed as a form of disenfranchisement, one in which the government deprives Americans of their right to self-defense. It makes sense that criminals are emboldened when they know that the general public is not allowed to carry guns—and in fact, this was the finding of a Justice Department study on what felons fear. As news correspondent John Stossel reports, "What felons fear most is not the police or the prison system, but their fellow citizens, who might be armed. One inmate told me, 'When you gonna rob somebody you don't know, it makes it harder because you don't know what to expect out of them.'" Incidentally, criminals will never abide by gun control laws—they acquire their weapons illegally and use them for illegal ends. Therefore, the only people who will be disarmed by gun control are law-abiding citizens—the very people whose hands we want and need guns to be in. "Disarming those who only want to defend themselves," write two attorneys who are intimately familiar with gun control, "is a surefire road to empowering criminals at the expense of the innocent" (Kates and Hehmeyer).

What is the topic sentence of Paragraph 3? What pieces of evidence are used to show that it is true?

The author quotes an expert who makes a point the author did not think of herself. The unique point helps support the author's other points.

Paragraph 4

What is the topic sentence of Paragraph 4? How did you recognize it?

Finally, gun control laws are a violation of the U.S. Constitution. The Second Amendment guarantees "the right of the people to keep and bear Arms" and makes it very clear that this right "shall not be infringed." The Second Amendment is as important as the other parts of the Constitution, which grant Americans the right to vote; the right to be punished humanely; and the right to a speedy and public trial, among others. No one would ever suggest limiting or restricting these rights! The Second Amendment is no different. Furthermore, the values and ideas enshrined in the Second Amendment are as valid and appropriate today as they were at the beginning of American history, and even more so. The breakdown of societal values and responsibility, the erosion of the nuclear family, and an increase in violent and disturbed tendencies makes the right to own a gun more critical than ever.

"Furthermore" is a transition. Make a list of all the transitions that appear in the essay and how they keep the ideas flowing.

Paragraph 5

Note how the author returns to ideas introduced in Paragraph 1. See Exercise 3A for more on introductions and conclusions.

After every senseless shooting, after every school massacre, the American public scratches its head, wondering how such a tragedy could have been prevented. The answer is right in front of us: Let the people arm themselves, and together we can actively prevent these horrible tragedies. As commentator Michelle Malkin has put it, a safer America "begins with renewing a culture of self-defense—mind, spirit and body. It begins with two words: Fight back." Curtailing our right to own guns makes America a more dangerous place and robs Americans of their constitutional rights and liberties—so let's fight back, against both criminals and politicians who want to impose gun control laws.

The author closes her essay with a call to action that is supposed to inspire the reader to do something about the problem discussed.

Works Cited

Kates, Don B., and Carol Hehmeyer. "Nation's Rates of Private Gun Ownership Do Not Correlate to Rates of Murder." *Daily Journal* Aug. 2007 < http://www.gunowners.org/op0746.htm > .

Malkin, Michelle. "Wanted: A Culture of Self-Defense." Townhall.com 18 Apr. 2007 < http://www.townhall.com/Columnist/MichelleMalkin/2007/04/18/wanted_a_culture_of_self_defense > .

Stossel, John. "Myths About Gun Control." RealClearPolitics.com 19 Oct. 2005 < http://www.realclearpolitics.com/Commentary/com-10_19_05_JS.html > .

Exercise 2A: Create an Outline from an Existing Essay

As you did for the first model essay in this section, create an outline that could have been used to write *The Consequences of Gun Control*. Be sure to identify the essay's thesis statement, its supporting ideas, its descriptive passages, and key pieces of evidence that were used.

Exercise 2B: Create an Outline for Your Own Essay

The second model essay expresses a particular point of view about gun control. For this exercise, your assignment is to find supporting ideas, choose specific and concrete details, create an outline, and ultimately write a five-paragraph essay making a different, or even opposing, point about gun control. Your goal is to use cause-and-effect techniques to convince your reader.

Step One: Write a thesis statement.
The following thesis statement would be appropriate for a multiple effects essay on benefits of gun control:

> **Limiting the number of guns in our society and putting restrictions on the way in which people are allowed to use guns is the only way we are going to become a safer, more peaceful nation.**

Or see the sample paper topics suggested in Appendix D for more ideas.

Step Two: Brainstorm pieces of supporting evidence.
Using information from some of the viewpoints in the previous section and from the information found in Section Three of this book, write down three arguments or pieces of evidence that support the thesis statement you selected. Then, for each of these three arguments, write down supportive facts, examples, and details that support it. These could be:

- statistical information
- personal memories and anecdotes

- quotes from experts, peers, or family members
- observations of people's actions and behaviors
- specific and concrete details

Supporting pieces of evidence for the above sample thesis statement are found in this book and include:

- Gun control measures described by Juliet A. Leftwich in Viewpoint Two that she claims are reasonable restrictions that will prevent guns from falling into the hands of criminals, the mentally ill, juveniles, and others who should not have access to guns.
- Quote from Viewpoint Three in which Jonathon Gatehouse, Michael Friscolanti, and Luiza C.H. Savage say, "It's hard to escape the conclusion that America's patchwork of loopholes and exceptions, stretched and warped by the endless battle over citizens' constitutional 'right' to bear arms, are at best ineffective, and at worst an act of national self-sabotage."
- Statistics in Appendix A on how many children a year are killed in gun accidents. This information could be used to counter claims that gun-related murders are the result of a disarmed citizenry.

Step Three: Place the information from Step Two in outline form.

Step Four: Write the arguments or supporting statements in paragraph form.

By now you have three arguments that support the paragraph's thesis statement, as well as supporting material. Use the outline to write out your three supporting arguments in paragraph form. Make sure each paragraph has a topic sentence that states the paragraph's thesis clearly and broadly. Then add supporting sentences that express the facts, quotes, details, and examples that support the paragraph's argument. The paragraph may also have a concluding or summary sentence.

Essay Three

The Making of a School Shooter

Editor's Notes The following essay illustrates the third type of cause-and-effect essay: a "chain of events" essay. In this kind of essay, each link in the chain is both the effect of what happened before and the cause of what happens next. In other words, instead of factors A, B, and C causing phenomenon X, the "chain of events" essay describes how A causes B, which then causes C, which in turn results in X. Specifically, the author examines the chain of events that led Seung-Hui Cho to kill thirty-two people at Virginia Polytechnic Institute and State University (Virginia Tech). Chronology—expressing which events come before and which after—plays an important part in this type of essay.

This essay also differs from the previous model essays in that it is longer than five paragraphs. Sometimes five paragraphs are simply not enough to adequately develop an idea. Extending the length of an essay can allow the reader to explore a topic in more depth or present multiple pieces of evidence that together provide a complete picture of a topic. Longer essays can also help readers discover the complexity of a subject by examining a topic beyond its superficial exterior. Moreover, the ability to write a longer research or position paper is a valuable skill you will need as you advance academically.

As you read, consider the questions posed in the margins. Continue to identify thesis statements, supporting details, transitions, and quotations. Examine the introductory and concluding paragraphs to understand how they give shape to the essay. Finally, evaluate the essay's general structure and assess its overall effectiveness.

Refers to thesis and topic sentences

Refers to supporting details

Paragraph 1

On April 16, 2007, Seung-Hui Cho killed thirty-two classmates and teachers at Virginia Tech University before turning the gun on himself. Americans have wondered

74

what could have caused a person to perpetrate the deadliest mass shooting in American history. A series of disturbing events reveal that Cho's shooting rampage was years in the making, the result of a chain reaction of mental, social, and developmental problems and a fascination with violence.

What is the essay's thesis statement? How did you recognize it?

Paragraph 2

Even as a child, Cho displayed odd characteristics that indicated his tendency toward the macabre. Those who knew him report he was a very quiet and shy child who did not like to play with others. Some family members suspected he might be mentally ill. Other family members described him as exceptionally cold, rarely making eye contact or engaging in physically intimate gestures such as hugs, even with the people to whom he was closest. According to his uncle, "'The kid didn't say much and didn't mix with other children. 'Yes sir' was about all you could get from him'" (qtd. in Kleinfeld). Elementary school officials diagnosed him early on as having both emotional and verbal developmental problems.

This is the topic sentence of Paragraph 2. Without reading the rest of the paragraph, take a guess at what the paragraph will be about.

What kinds of voices are quoted in the essay? Make a list of everyone quoted, along with their credentials.

Paragraph 3

Over time, Cho's abnormal social interactions caused mental health authorities to take notice. At one point Cho was diagnosed with major depression and a condition called "selective mutism," a disorder in which a person chooses not to speak. Records show he took Paxil, an antidepressant, for one year. While Cho was in high school, his parents took him to counseling once a week. But once he entered college, he failed to keep up with counseling on his own, and the university health system failed to provide him with the help he needed. Wrote one reporter of Cho's mental illness, "When Cho left his home in Washington, D.C.'s Virginia suburbs, he appeared to be a young man who had overcome mental illness with the help of medication, counseling and the support of his family and his schools. . . . But in college, Cho's illness went untreated, and school officials repeatedly missed

What words and phrases indicate this is a cause-and-effect essay?

the warning signs that he was a danger" (Moran). In 2005 Cho was deemed to be mentally ill by the New River Valley Community Services Board, which recommended that he be hospitalized. He was judged by several different mental health authorities to be a danger to himself and/or others, but little action was taken.

Paragraph 4

What is the topic sentence of paragraph 4? How does it relate to the essay's thesis?

At Virginia Tech, Cho's mental and social problems caused him to be socially isolated, and he made few friends. Most of his classmates and roommates remember him as being an odd person wno was extremely quiet—he would rarely answer people even if they spoke directly to him. A few people felt threatened by him: Two female students on campus, for example, reported him to the police after he repeatedly called, visited, and instant-messaged them. Others remembered him as being delusional, reporting that he made up a supermodel girlfriend named Jelly who lived in outer space. Another fabricated story he told featured a vacation he took with Vladmir Putin, the former president of Russia.

These specific details help you picture what kind of student Cho was. Always use specific rather than vague details when writing.

Paragraph 5

In what way does paragraph 5 represent a "link" in the "chain of events"?

Though Cho was known for being incredibly quiet, his rapidly worsening mental condition led him to express himself through another medium: writing. Cho became known by fellow English classmates for writing extremely creepy and gory stories and plays. In a play titled *Richard McBeef*, Cho wrote about a teenager who threatens to kill his stepfather. In another, *Mr. Brownstone*, two friends fantasize about killing their math teacher. Steven Davis, a classmate of Cho's, said that after he read *Richard McBeef* he turned to his roommate and said, "This is the kind of guy who is going to walk into a classroom and start shooting people" (qtd. in Kleinfeld).

Analyze this quote. What do you think made the author want to select it for inclusion in the essay?

Paragraph 6

That's exactly what Cho started to plan for beginning in February 2007, when records show he ordered a gun from an online dealer. In March 2007 he bought a second gun and fifty rounds of ammunition, and he began visiting a shooting range for practice. Through April 13 he continued to purchase more rounds of ammunition, along with cargo pants, sunglasses, gloves, and a hunting knife. In all, Cho spent several thousands of dollars preparing for the massacre. He also made changes to his physical appearance: His roommates reported that several weeks before the shootings he cut his hair very short and began working out regularly at a nearby gym.

Paragraph 7

It is unknown why Cho selected April 16 as the day for his awful massacre. His roommate remembered that he awoke unusually early that morning, around 5 A.M. Only Cho knows exactly what happened next, but authorities have been able to piece together a general timeline of the events. Cho first went to West Ambler Johnston Hall, where he shot and killed two people at around 7:15 A.M. Then he returned to his dorm room, assembled a package of photos, videos, and an eighteen-hundred-word document and took it to the post office, where he mailed it at 9:01 A.M. to NBC news. He then returned to his dorm room, rearmed himself, and headed to Norris Hall, where he killed twenty-five students and five teachers in five different classrooms, all before killing himself at around 10 A.M.

"Only Cho knows exactly what happened next" is a transitional phrase that lets you know cause-and-effect relationship is being established. What other transitional words and phrases common to cause-and-effect essays are found in this essay?

Paragraph 8

In addition to being mentally ill and delusional, it is possible that Cho's disdain for the privileged, wealthy students at Virginia Tech played a motivating factor in his decision to kill. In the package sent to NBC news, Cho included a videotaped message in which he ranted about his hatred for spoiled, rich, college kids, indicating that the behavior and status of his schoolmates had somehow driven him to murder them. "You had a hundred billion chances and ways to have avoided today," he said in the tape. "But you decided to spill my blood. You forced me into a corner and gave me only one option. The decision was yours. Now you have blood on your hands that will never wash off" (qtd. in Welch).

How is the topic of Paragraph 8 different from, but related to, the other topics discussed thus far?

This type of quote is a *primary source* because it features the words of the essay's subject: Cho. A primary source enlivens an essay in many ways, and in this case offers a chilling, first-hand account of the subject.

After the Virginia Tech massacre, a former classmate of Cho's said, "Looking back, he fit the exact stereotype of what one would typically think of as a 'school shooter'— a loner, obsessed with violence, and serious personal problems" (MacFarlane). Despite the signs, no person or authority was able to predict that Cho would one day become the perpetrator of the worst school shooting— and the worst massacre—in American history. While understanding the chain of events that led him to murder so many innocent people offers insight into the development of a school shooter, it can never lessen the pain and shock of such a tragic event.

Note how the author returns to ideas introduced in Paragraph 1. See Exercise 3A for more on introductions and conclusions.

Works Cited

Kleinfeld, N.R. "Before Deadly Rage, a Life Consumed by a Troubling Silence." *New York Times* 22 Apr 2007 < http://www.nytimes.com/2007/04/22/us/22vatech.html?_r = 1&adxnnl = 1&oref = slogin &adxnnlx = 1212426334-zn ex5orF + HEOQ7yd9tuEtQ > .

MacFarlane, Ian. "Cho Seung-Hui's Plays." AOL News Bloggers 17 Apr. 2007 < http://news.aol.com/news-bloggers/2007/04/17/cho-seung-huis-plays/ > .

Moran, Terry. "Inside Cho's Mind: Report Shows Virginia Tech Made Mistakes." ABC News 30 Aug. 2007 < http://abc news.go.com/Nightline/Story?id = 3541157&page = 3 > .

Welch, William M. "Va. Tech Gunman Sent Material to NBC." *USA Today* 18 Apr. 2007 < http://www.usatoday. com/news/nation/2007-04-18-virginia-tech_N.htm > .

Exercise 3A: Examining Introductions and Conclusions

Every essay features introductory and concluding paragraphs that are used to frame the main ideas being presented. Along with presenting the essay's thesis statement, well-written introductions should grab the attention of the reader and make clear why the topic being explored is important. The conclusion reiterates the essay's thesis and is also the last chance for the writer to make an impression on the reader. Strong introductions and conclusions can greatly enhance an essay's effect on an audience.

The Introduction

There are several techniques that can be used to craft an introductory paragraph. An essay can start with

- an anecdote: a brief story that illustrates a point relevant to the topic;
- startling information: facts or statistics that elucidate the point of the essay;
- setting up and knocking down a position: a position or claim believed by proponents of one side of a controversy, followed by statements that challenge that claim;
- historical perspective: an example of the way things used to be that leads into a discussion of how or why things work differently now;
- summary information: general introductory information about the topic that feeds into the essay's thesis statement.

1. Reread the introductory paragraphs of the model essays and of the viewpoints in Section One. Identify which of the techniques described above are used in the example essays. How do they grab the attention of the reader? Are their thesis statements clearly presented?

2. Write an introduction for the essay you have outlined and partially written in Exercise 2B using one of the techniques described above.

The Conclusion

The conclusion brings the essay to a close by summarizing or returning to its main ideas. Good conclusions, however, go beyond simply repeating these ideas. Strong conclusions explore a topic's broader implications and reiterate why it is important to consider. They may frame the essay by returning to an anecdote featured in the opening paragraph. Or they may close with a quotation or refer back to an event in the essay. In opinionated essays, the conclusion can reiterate which side the essay is taking or ask the reader to reconsider a previously held position on the subject.

3. Reread the concluding paragraphs of the model essays and of the viewpoints in Section One. Which were most effective in driving their arguments home to the reader? What sorts of techniques did they use to do this? Did they appeal emotionally to the reader or bookend an idea or event referenced elsewhere in the essay?

4. Write a conclusion for the essay you have outlined and partially written in Exercise 2B using one of the techniques described above.

Exercise 3B: Using Quotations to Enliven Your Essay

No essay is complete without quotations. Get in the habit of using quotes to support at least some of the ideas in your essays. Quotes do not need to appear in every paragraph, but they should be used often enough so that the essay contains voices aside from your own. When you write, use quotations to accomplish the following:

- Provide expert advice that you are not necessarily in a position to know about.
- Cite lively or passionate passages.
- Include a particularly well-written point that gets to the heart of the matter.
- Supply statistics or facts that have been derived from someone's research.
- Deliver anecdotes that illustrate the point you are trying to make.
- Express first-person testimony.

Problem One:

Reread the essays presented in all sections of this book and find at least one example of each of the above quotation types.

There are a couple of important things to remember when using quotations:

- Note your sources' qualifications and biases. This way your reader can identify the person you have quoted and can put their words in a context.
- Put any quoted material within proper quotation marks. Failing to attribute quotes to their authors constitutes plagiarism, which is when an author takes someone else's words or ideas and presents them as his or her own. Plagiarism is a very serious infraction and must be avoided at all costs.

Write Your Own Cause-and-Effect Five-Paragraph Essay

Using the information from this book, write your own five-paragraph cause-and-effect essay that deals with gun control. You can use the resources in this book for information about issues relating to gun control and how to structure a cause-and-effect essay.

The following steps are suggestions on how to get started.

Step One: Choose your topic.

The first step is to decide what topic to write your cause-and-effect essay on. Is there any subject that particularly fascinates you? Is there an issue you strongly support or feel strongly against? Is there a topic you feel personally connected to? Ask yourself such questions before selecting your essay topic. Refer to Appendix D: Sample Essay Topics if you need help selecting a topic.

Step Two: Write down questions and answers about the topic.

Before you begin writing, you will need to think carefully about what ideas your essay will contain. This is a process known as *brainstorming*. Brainstorming involves asking yourself questions and coming up with ideas to discuss in your essay. Possible questions that will help you with the brainstorming process include:

- Why is this topic important?
- Why should people be interested in this topic?
- How can I make this essay interesting to the reader?
- What question am I going to address in this paragraph or essay?
- What facts, ideas, or quotes can I use to support the answer to my question?

Questions especially for cause-and-effect essays include:

- What are the causes of the topic being examined?
- What are the effects of the topic being examined?

- Are there single or multiple causes?
- Are there single or multiple effects?
- Is a chain reaction or domino series of events involved?

Step Three: Gather facts, ideas, and anecdotes related to your topic.

This book contains several places to find information, including the viewpoints and the appendices. In addition, you may want to research the books, articles, and Web sites listed in Section Three or do additional research in your local library. You can also conduct interviews if you know someone who has a compelling story that would fit well in your essay.

Step Four: Develop a workable thesis statement.

Use what you have written down in steps two and three to help you articulate the main point or argument you want to make in your essay. It should be expressed in a clear sentence and make an arguable or supportable point.

Example:

The framers of the Constitution never intended school shootings and armed robberies to result from the "right to keep and bear arms."

> This could be the thesis statement of a cause-and-effect essay that argues that the Second Amendment does not grant private citizens the right to own handguns and that gun ownership causes unnecessary murder and violence in America.

Step Five: Write an outline or diagram.
1. Write the thesis statement at the top of the outline.
2. Write roman numerals I, II, and III on the left side of the page, with A, B, and C under each numeral.
3. Next to each roman numeral, write down the best ideas you came up with in step three. These should all directly relate to and support the thesis statement.

4. Next to each letter, write down information that supports that particular idea.

Step Six: Write the three supporting paragraphs.
Use your outline to write the three supporting paragraphs. Write down the main idea of each paragraph in sentence form. Do the same thing for the supporting points of information. Each sentence should support the topic of the paragraph. Be sure you have relevant and interesting details, facts, and quotes. Use transitions when you move from idea to idea to keep the text fluid and smooth. Sometimes, although not always, paragraphs can include a concluding or summary sentence that restates the paragraph's argument.

Step Seven: Write the introduction and conclusion.
See Exercise 3A for information on writing introductions and conclusions.

Step Eight: Read and rewrite.
As you read, check your essay for the following:

- ✔ Does the essay maintain a consistent tone?
- ✔ Do all paragraphs reinforce your general thesis?
- ✔ Do all paragraphs flow from one to the other? Do you need to add transition words or phrases?
- ✔ Have you quoted from reliable, authoritative, and interesting sources?
- ✔ Is there a sense of progression throughout the essay?
- ✔ Does the essay get bogged down in too much detail or irrelevant material?
- ✔ Does your introduction grab the reader's attention?
- ✔ Does your conclusion reflect on any previously discussed material or give the essay a sense of closure?
- ✔ Are there any spelling or grammatical errors?

Section Three: Supporting Research Material

Facts About Gun Control

Editor's Note: These facts can be used in reports or papers to reinforce or add credibility when making important points or claims.

Important Dates in Gun Control

1791
The Second Amendment is ratified, giving "the right of the people to keep and bear arms."

1934
In an attempt to curb the activities of gangsters like John Dillinger and Al Capone, the National Firearms Act imposes a tax on the sale and transfer of machine guns and short-barrel firearms, including sawed-off shotguns.

1938
The Federal Firearms Act requires federal licensing of gun dealers.

1968
The Gun Control Act is expanded after John F. Kennedy, Robert Kennedy, and Martin Luther King Jr. are assassinated. It is updated to prohibit felons and the mentally ill from buying guns and bans the sale of mail-order firearms, including rifles and shotguns.

1972
The Bureau of Alcohol, Tobacco, and Firearms is created to oversee the regulation of gun sales.

1986
The Firearms Owners Protection Act is passed. It eases some gun sale restrictions and bars the government from creating a database of gun dealer records. It also authorizes the sale of guns between private owners.

Commentators say the law reflects the growing influence of the National Rifle Association and the strongly pro-gun administration of President Ronald Reagan.

1993

The Brady Handgun Violence Prevention Act is passed. Named for James Brady, the press secretary disabled by the attempted assassination of President Reagan in 1981, it requires gun dealers—although not private sellers—to run background checks on purchasers and authorizes the creation of a national database.

1994

The Violent Crime Control and Law Enforcement Act is passed. It bans the sale of new assault weapons for ten years.

2003

In the wake of a wave of lawsuits against gun dealers, Congress protects gun manufacturers and dealers from lawsuits if their guns are used in crimes.

2004

The assault weapons ban expires and is not renewed by Congress.

2007

After the massacre at Virginia Tech in which thirty-three people were killed, Congress closes a loophole in the National Instant Criminal Background Check System by requiring states to automate lists of people prohibited from buying firearms, including felons and the mentally ill, and put them in the federal database.

2008

The Supreme Court rules in *District of Columbia v. Heller* that the Second Amendment does indeed protect an individual's right to possess a firearm for private use.

Guns and Crime in America

According to the Bureau of Justice Statistics:

- Less than 10 percent of nonfatal violent crimes have involved a firearm since 1996.
- Incidents involving a firearm represented 9 percent of the 4.7 million violent crimes of rape and sexual assault, robbery, and aggravated and simple assault in 2005.
- The percentage of homicide victims killed with a gun increases with age up to age seventeen and declines thereafter.
- Guns are most often used when people in close relationships kill each other. Between 1990 and 2005:
  - Over two-thirds of spouse and ex-spouse victims were killed by guns.
  - 69 percent of men murdered by their spouse were killed with guns.
  - 86 percent of men murdered by their ex-spouse were killed with guns.
  - 68 percent of women murdered by their spouse were killed with guns.
  - 77 percent of women murdered by their ex-spouse were killed with guns.
  - 45 percent of men murdered by their girlfriends were killed with guns.
  - 56 percent of women murdered by their boyfriends were killed with guns.

The FBI estimates that 66 percent of the 16,137 murders in 2004 were committed with firearms.

According to the National Crime Victimization Survey (NCVS) in 2005, 477,040 victims of violent crimes stated that they faced an offender with a firearm.

According to Americans for Gun Safety, gun theft is most likely in states without laws requiring safe storage of firearms in the home and where there are large numbers of gun owners and relatively high crime rates.

According to the FBI, nearly 1.7 million guns were reported stolen between 1995 and 2005, and only 40 percent of those were recovered. More than 80 percent of these guns were taken from homes or cars.

Most law enforcement officers are killed with firearms, particularly handguns.

According to the Coalition to Stop Gun Violence, more than eighty Americans die from gun violence each day.

According to Americans for Gun Safety, twenty of the nation's twenty-two national gun laws are not enforced.

According to U.S. Department of Justice data, only 2 percent of federal gun crimes are actually prosecuted.

Children and Guns

The Brady Center reports:

- In 2004 nearly eight young people aged nineteen and under were killed each day by a firearm in the United States.
- In 2005 nearly forty-five young people aged nineteen and under were nonfatally wounded each day.
- In 2004, 1,804 children and teenagers were murdered in gun homicides, 846 committed suicide with guns, and 143 died in unintentional shootings.
- In 2004 a total of 2,852 young people were killed by firearms in the United States, one every three hours.
- In 2004, 82 percent of murder victims aged thirteen to nineteen were killed with a firearm.
- During 2004, 55 percent of all murders of those under age eighteen in the United States involved firearms.
- Firearms are the second leading cause of death (after motor vehicle accidents) for young people nineteen and under in the United States.

- The rate of firearm death of under fourteen-year-olds is nearly twelve times higher in the United States than in twenty-five other industrialized countries combined.
- In 2004, for every child and teenager killed by a gun, nearly five were estimated to be nonfatally wounded.
- From 1999 to 2004, firearms were responsible for 18 percent of injury deaths for Caucasian teens aged thirteen to nineteen in the United States, 51 percent of deaths for African American teens, 31 percent of Hispanic teens, 18 percent of Native American/Alaska Native teens, and 19 percent of Asian/Pacific Islander teens.
- In a study of inner-city seven-year-olds and their exposure to violence, 75 percent of them reported hearing gunshots.

The American Medical Association reports that between 36 percent and 50 percent of male eleventh graders believe that they could easily get a gun if they wanted one.

According to a report by the Josephson Institute of Ethics, 60 percent of high school and 31 percent of middle school boys said they could get a gun if they wanted to.

According to the Centers for Disease Control and Prevention:
- The rate of firearm deaths among kids under age fifteen is almost twelve times higher in the United States than in twenty-five other industrialized countries combined.
- American kids are sixteen times more likely to be murdered with a gun, eleven times more likely to commit suicide with a gun, and nine times more likely to die from a firearm accident than children in twenty-five other industrialized countries combined.

American Opinions About Guns and Gun Control

A 2007 Fox News poll found that:

- About one of five Americans (19 percent) believes tougher gun laws can help stop mass shootings like the one at Virginia Tech.
- 71 percent of Americans believe tougher gun laws cannot help prevent mass shootings.
- 78 percent of gun owners and 64 percent of non-gun-owners believe that tougher gun laws will not prevent crime, because criminals will always find ways around gun laws.

According to a 2008 poll by the Pew Research Center:

- 36 percent of Americans favor laws that would ban the sale of handguns; 59 percent oppose them.
- 37 percent of Americans think it is more important to protect the right of Americans to own guns rather than control gun ownership; 58 percent think it is more important to control gun ownership rather than to protect the right of Americans to own guns.

According to a February 2008 *USA Today*/Gallup poll:

- 49 percent of Americans would like to see gun control laws made stricter; 11 percent would like to see them made less strict; 38 percent believe they should remain as they are; and 2 percent are undecided.
- 73 percent of Americans believe the Second Amendment guarantees Americans the right to own guns.
- 20 percent believe the Second Amendment guarantees only members of state militias such as the National Guard the right to own guns.

A 2007 Gallup poll found that about 42 percent of Americans keep a gun in their home; about 57 percent do not.

According to a 2007 ABC News poll:

- 55 percent of Americans support a nationwide ban on semiautomatic handguns.
- 67 percent of Americans support a ban on the sale of assault weapons.
- 55 percent of Americans oppose a ban on carrying a concealed weapon.
- 60 percent of Americans oppose a ban on the sale of handguns to anyone but law enforcement officers.
- 40 percent of Americans blame pop culture for gun violence in America.
- 35 percent of Americans blame poor parenting for gun violence in America.
- 18 percent of Americans blame the availability of guns for gun violence in America.
- 5 percent and 2 percent respectively blame other causes or are unsure.

Finding and Using Sources of Information

No matter what type of essay you are writing, it is necessary to find information to support your point of view. You can use sources such as books, magazine articles, newspaper articles, and online articles.

Using Books and Articles

You can find books and articles in a library by using the library's computer or cataloging system. If you are not sure how to use these resources, ask a librarian to help you. You can also use a computer to find many magazine articles and other articles written specifically for the Internet.

You are likely to find a lot more information than you can possibly use in your essay, so your first task is to narrow it down to what is likely to be most usable. Look at book and article titles. Look at book chapter titles, and examine the book's index to see if it contains information on the specific topic you want to write about. (For example, if you want to write about right-to-carry laws and you find a book about gun control in general, check the chapter titles and index to be sure it contains information about right-to-carry laws specifically before you bother to check out the book.)

For a five-paragraph essay, you do not need a great deal of supporting information, so quickly try to narrow down your materials to a few good books and magazine or Internet articles. You do not need dozens. You might even find that one or two good books or articles contain all the information you need.

You probably do not have time to read an entire book, so find the chapters or sections that relate to your topic and skim these. When you find useful information, copy it onto a note card or into a notebook. You should look for supporting facts, statistics, quotations, and examples.

Using the Internet

When you select your supporting information, it is important that you evaluate its source. This is especially important with information you find on the Internet. Because nearly anyone can put information on the Internet, there is as much bad information as good information. Before using Internet information—or any information—try to determine if the source seems to be reliable. Is the author or Internet site sponsored by a legitimate organization? Is it from a government source? Does the author have any special knowledge or training related to the topic you are looking up? Does the article give any indication of where its information comes from?

Using Your Supporting Information

When you use supporting information from a book, article, interview or other source, there are three important things to remember:

1. *Make it clear whether you are using a direct quotation or a paraphrase*. If you copy information directly from your source, you are quoting it. You must put quotation marks around the information and tell where the information comes from. If you put the information in your own words, you are paraphrasing it.

Here is an example of a using a quotation:

While law-abiding citizens are likely to abide by gun control laws, criminals are not. Therefore, as two lawyers with expert knowledge on the subject argue, "Banning guns to the general public increases people's vulnerability and fails to reduce violence because the law-abiding citizenry are victims of violent crime, not perpetrators" (Kates and Hehmeyer).

Here is an example of a brief paraphrase of the same passage:

> While law-abiding citizens are likely to abide by gun control laws, criminals are not. Given this, attorneys Don B. Kates and Carol Hehmeyer have warned that banning or restricting gun ownership threatens law-abiding citizens who will comply with laws to disarm, making them vulnerable to criminals who will continue to illegally arm themselves.

2. *Use the information fairly.* Be careful to use supporting information in the way the author intended it. For example, it is unfair to quote an author as saying, "Guns are safe when in the right hands," when he or she intended to say, "Guns are safe when in the right hands, but since one cannot control in whose hands a gun will end up, it is better to take away all of them." This is called taking information out of context. This practice uses supporting evidence unfairly.

3. *Give credit where credit is due.* Giving credit is known as citing. You must use citations when you use someone else's information, but not every piece of supporting information needs a citation.

   - If the supporting information is general knowledge—that is, it can be found in many sources—you do not have to cite your source.
   - If you directly quote a source, you must cite it.
   - If you paraphrase information from a specific source, you must cite it.

If you do not use citations where you should, you are *plagiarizing*—or stealing—someone else's work.

Citing Your Sources

There are a number of ways to cite your sources. Your teacher will probably want you to do it in one of three ways:

- Informal: As in the example in number 1 above, tell where you got the information as you present it in the text of your essay.
- Informal list: At the end of your essay, place an unnumbered list of all the sources you used. This tells the reader where, in general, your information came from.
- Formal: Use numbered footnotes or endnotes. Footnotes or endnotes are generally placed at the end of an article or essay, although they may be placed elsewhere depending on your teacher's requirements.

Works Cited

Kates, Don B. and Carol Hehmeyer. "Nation's Rates of Private Gun Ownership Do Not Correlate to Rates of Murder." *Daily Journal* Aug 2007.

Using MLA Style to Create a Works Cited List

You will probably need to create a list of works cited for your paper. These include materials that you quoted from, relied heavily on, or consulted to write your paper. There are several different ways to structure these references. The following examples are based on Modern Language Association (MLA) style, one of the major citation styles used by writers.

Book Entries

For most book entries you will need the author's name, the book's title, where it was published, what company published it, and the year it was published. This information is usually found on the inside of the book. Variations on book entries include the following:

A book by a single author:
> Simon, Jonathan. *Governing Through Crime: How the War on Crime Transformed American Democracy and Created a Culture of Fear*. New York: Oxford University Press, 2007.

Two or more books by the same author:
> Mernissi, Fatima. *Beyond the Veil*. San Francisco: Saqi Books, 2003.
> ———. *Fear of the Modern World*. New York: Basic Books, 2002.

A book by two or more authors:
> Esposito, John L., and Dalia Mogahed. *Who Speaks for Islam? What a Billion Muslims Really Think*. Washington, DC: Gallup Press, 2008.

A book with an editor:
>Friedman, Lauri S., ed. *Writing the Critical Essay: Democracy.* Farmington Hills, MI: Greenhaven, 2008.

Periodical and Newspaper Entries

Entries for sources found in periodicals and newspapers are cited a bit differently than books. For one, these sources usually have a title and a publication name. They also may have specific dates and page numbers. Unlike book entries, you do not need to list where newspapers or periodicals are published or what company publishes them.

An article from a periodical:
>Bauer, Henry H. "The Mystery of HIV/AIDS." *Quadrant* Jul.–Aug. 2006: 61–64.

An unsigned article from a periodical:
>"The Chinese Disease? The Rapid Spread of Syphilis in China." *Global Agenda* 14 Jan. 2007.

An article from a newspaper:
>Bradsher, Keith. "A New, Global Oil Quandary: Costly Fuel Means Costly Calories." *New York Times* 19 Jan. 2008: A2.

Internet Sources

To document a source you found online, try to provide as much information on it as possible, including the author's name, the title of the document, date of publication or of last revision, the URL, and your date of access.

A Web source:
>Butts, Jeffrey. "Too Many Youths Facing Adult Justice." Urban Institute. 25 Aug. 2004 < http:// www.urban.org/publications/900728.html >.

Your teacher will tell you exactly how information should be cited in your essay. Generally, the very least information needed is the original author's name and the name of the article or other publication.

Be sure you know exactly what information your teacher requires before you start looking for your supporting information so that you know what information to include with your notes.

Sample Essay Topics

People Should Have the Right to Own Guns

People Should Not Have the Right to Own Guns

People Should Have the Right to Carry a Concealed Weapon

People Should Not Have the Right to Carry a Concealed Weapon

Gun Ownership Is a Public Health Hazard

Gun Ownership Is Not a Public Health Hazard

Handguns Should Be Banned

Handguns Should Not Be Banned

Gun Ownership Is Protected by the Second Amendment

Gun Ownership Is Not Protected by the Second Amendment

Gun Control Is Unconstitutional

Gun Control Is Constitutional

Guns Are an Effective Means of Self-Defense

Guns Are Not an Effective Means of Self-Defense

Gun Manufacturers Should Be Held Responsible for Gun Violence

Gun Manufacturers Should Not Be Held Responsible for Gun Violence

Gun Safety Standards Should Be Mandatory

Gun Safety Standards Should Not Be Mandatory

Students Should Be Allowed to Bring Guns to School

Students Should Not Be Allowed to Bring Guns to School

Guns Should Be Allowed in the Workplace

Guns Should Not Be Allowed in the Workplace

Topics for Cause-and-Effect Essays

Gun Control Causes Violence and Crime

Gun Control Prevents Violence and Crime

The Right to Shoot in Self-Defense Can Reduce Violence

The Right to Shoot in Self-Defense Cannot Reduce Violence

Legalizing Concealed Weapons Makes Society Safer

Legalizing Concealed Weapons Does Not Make Society Safer

"Smart Guns" Can Prevent Violence and Crime

"Smart Guns" Cannot Prevent Violence and Crime

Gun Control Can Prevent School Shootings

Gun Control Cannot Prevent School Shootings

Armed Security Guards Can Prevent School Shootings

Armed Security Guards Cannot Prevent School Shootings

Organizations to Contact

American Civil Liberties Union (ACLU)
125 Broad St., 18th Flr., New York, NY 10004
(212) 549-2500 • e-mail: aclu@aclu.org
Web site: www.aclu.org

The ACLU champions the rights set forth in the Declaration of Independence and the U.S. Constitution. It interprets the Second Amendment as a guarantee for states to form militias, not as a guarantee of the individual right to own and bear firearms. Consequently, the organization believes that gun control is constitutional and necessary.

The Brady Center to Prevent Handgun Violence
1225 Eye St. NW, Ste. 1100, Washington, DC 20005
(202) 289-7319 • fax: (202) 408-1851
Web sites: www.cphv.org • www.gunlawsuits.org

The center is the legal action, research, and education affiliate of Handgun Control, Inc. The center's Legal Action Project provides free legal representation for victims in lawsuits against reckless gun manufacturers, dealers, and owners.

Canadian Coalition for Gun Control
PO Box 90062, 1488 Queen St. West, Toronto, ON M6K 3K3
(416) 604-0209 • Web site: www.guncontrol.ca

The coalition was formed to reduce gun death, injury, and crime. It supports the registration of all guns and works for tougher restrictions on handguns. The organization promotes safe storage requirements for all firearms and educates to counter the romance of guns. Various fact sheets and other educational materials on gun control are available on its Web site.

Citizens Committee for the Right to Keep and Bear Arms
12500 NE Tenth Pl., Bellevue, WA 98005
(425) 454-4911 • Web site: www.ccrkba.org

The committee believes that the U.S. Constitution's Second Amendment guarantees and protects the right of individual Americans to own guns. It works to educate the public concerning this right and to lobby legislators to prevent the passage of gun-control laws.

Coalition to Stop Gun Violence

1023 Fifteenth St. NW, Ste. 301, Washington, DC 20005
(202) 408-0061 • Web site: www.csgv.org

The coalition lobbies at the local, state, and federal levels to ban the sale of handguns and assault weapons to individuals and to institute licensing and registration of all firearms. It also litigates cases against firearms makers.

Gun Owners of America (GOA)

8001 Forbes Pl., Ste. 102, Springfield, VA 22151
(703) 321-8585
e-mail: goamail@gunowners.org • Web site: www.gunowners.org

This lobbying organization supports the ownership of guns as an issue of personal freedom and is dedicated to protecting and defending the Second Amendment rights of gun owners. Its online resources include the newsletter *The Gunowners*, gun control fact sheets, and information about firearms legislation in Congress.

Independence Institute

13952 Denver West Pkwy., Ste. 400, Golden, CO 80401
(303) 279-6536 • Web site: www.i2i.org

The Independence Institute is a think tank that supports gun ownership as a civil liberty and a constitutional right. Its publications include articles and booklets opposing gun control, many of which are found on its Web site.

Jews for the Preservation of Firearms Ownership (JPFO)

PO Box 270143, Hartford, WI 53027
(262) 673-9745 • e-mail: jpfo@jpfo.org
Web site: www.jpfo.org

JPFO is an organization that believes Jewish law mandates self-defense. Its primary goal is the elimination of the idea that gun control is a socially useful public policy.

Join Together
One Appleton St., 4th Flr., Boston, MA 02116-5223
(617) 437-1500 • e-mail: info@jointogether.org
Web site: www.jointogether.org

Join Together, a project of the Boston University School of Public Health, is an organization that serves as a national resource for communities working to reduce substance abuse and gun violence.

Million Mom March
1225 Eye St. NW, Ste. 1100, Washington, DC 20005
(888) 989-MOMS • Web site: www.millionmommarch.org

The foundation is a grassroots organization that supports commonsense gun laws. The foundation organized the Million Mom March, in which thousands marched through Washington, D.C., on Mother's Day, May 14, 2000, in support of licensing and registration and other firearms regulations.

National Crime Prevention Council (NCPC)
1000 Connecticut Ave. NW, 13th Flr., Washington, DC 20036
(202) 466-6272 • Web site: www.ncpc.org

The NCPC is a branch of the U.S. Department of Justice. Through its programs and education materials, the council works to teach Americans how to reduce crime and to address its causes. It provides readers with information on gun control and gun violence.

National Rifle Association (NRA)
11250 Waples Mill Rd., Fairfax, VA 22030
(703) 267-1000 • Web site: www.nra.org

With nearly 3 million members, the NRA is America's largest organization of gun owners. The NRA believes that gun control laws violate the U.S. Constitution and do not reduce crime.

Second Amendment Foundation

12500 NE Tenth Pl., Bellevue, WA 98005
(425) 454-7012 • Web site: www.saf.org

The foundation is dedicated to informing Americans about their Second Amendment right to keep and bear firearms. The foundation publishes numerous books, including *The Best Defense: True Stories of Intended Victims Who Defended Themselves with a Firearm* and *CCW: Carrying Concealed Weapons.* The complete text of the book *How to Defend Your Gun Rights* is available on its Web site.

Second Amendment Research Center

The John Glenn Institute, 350 Page Hall, 1810 College Rd.
Columbus, OH 43210
(614) 247-6371 • e-mail: 2nd-amend@osu.edu
Web site: www.secondamendmentcenter.org

Based at the John Glenn Institute for Public Service and Public Policy at Ohio State University, the center's goals are to examine how gun violence can be reduced while protecting the rights of gun owners. The organization's Web site is an excellent resource that includes a listing of articles by experts on both sides of the issue.

Violence Policy Center

1730 Rhode Island Ave. NW, Ste. 1014, Washington, DC 20036
(202) 822-8200 • e-mail: info@vpc.org
Web site: www.vpc.org

The center is an educational foundation that conducts research on firearms violence. It works to educate the public concerning the dangers of guns and supports gun-control measures. The center's publications include the reports *Safe at Home: How DC's Gun Laws Save Children's Lives; An Analysis of the Decline in Gun Dealers: 1994 to 2005;* and *Really Big Guns, Even Bigger Lies.*

Bibliography

Books

Bird, Chris, *Thank God I Had a Gun: True Accounts of Self-Defense*. San Antonio, TX: Privateer, 2006.

Carter, Gregg Lee, ed., *Gun Control in the United States: A Reference Handbook*. Santa Barbara, CA: ABC-CLIO, 2006.

Cornell, Saul, *A Well-Regulated Militia: The Founding Fathers and the Origin of Gun Control in America*. Oxford University Press, 2006.

Cukier, Wendy, and Victor W. Sidel, *The Global Gun Epidemic: From Saturday Night Specials to AK-47s*. Westport, CT: Praeger Security International, 2006.

Feldman, Richard, *Ricochet: Confessions of a Gun Lobbyist*. New York: Wiley, 2007.

Goss, Kristin A., *Disarmed: The Missing Movement for Gun Control in America*. Princeton, NJ: Princeton University Press, 2006.

Gottlieb, Alan, and Dave Workman, *America Fights Back: Armed Self-Defense in a Violent Age*. Bellevue, WA: Merrill, 2007.

Hutchinson, Gordon, and Todd Masson, *The Great New Orleans Gun Grab*. Boutte, LA: Louisiana Publishing, 2007.

Wilson, Harry L., *Guns, Gun Control, and Elections: The Politics and Policy of Firearms*. Lanham, MD: Rowman & Littlefield, 2006.

Periodicals

Boosler, Elayne, "We Are Getting Tired of Prying Your Guns Out of Your Cold Dead Hand," Huffington Post. com, April 18, 2007. www.huffingtonpost.com/elayne-boosler/we-are-getting-tired-of-p_b_46196.html.

Brady Center to Prevent Gun Violence, "No Gun Left Behind: The Gun Lobby's Campaign to Push Guns into Colleges and Schools." May 10, 2007. www.bradycenter.org/xshare/pdf/reports/no-gun-left-behind.pdf.

Durston, Bill, "It's the Guns," *Sacramento News and Review*, April 26, 2007.

Economist, "America's Tragedy: After the Virginia Tech Massacre," April 21, 2007, p. 11.

English, Merle, "A Woman's Crusade to Stop Gun Violence," *Newsday*, January 8, 2006.

Gaines, Patrice, "Violence Can't Be the Norm," *Washington Informer*, vol. 44, no. 7, December 6–December 12, 2007, pp. 21–22.

Gallagher, Mike, "Preventing Another Massacre," Townhall.com, April 20, 2007. http://mikegallagher.townhall.com/columnists/MikeGallagher/2007/04/20/preventing_another_massacre.

Greenhouse, Linda, "Do You Have a Right to 'Bear Arms'?" *New York Times Upfront*. January 14, 2008, p. 14.

Hagin, Doug, "How to Stop School Shootings?" Renew America.com, March 22, 2005. www.renewamerica.us/columns/hagin/050322.

Howe, Darcus, "Blair and the Guns That Kill Our Sons," *New Statesman* (1996), May 21, 2007, p. 22.

Judy, Karen, "Preventing Gun Violence: We Must Act," *Clinical Psychiatry News*, July 2007, p. 9.

Kates, Don B., "Understanding the Second: How the Bill of Rights Shaped Today's Gun Rights Debate," *Handguns*, April–May 2008, p. 14.

Lott, John R., Jr., "D.C.'s Flawed Reasoning; The City's Handgun Ban Doesn't Save Lives," *Washington Times*, September 7, 2007, p. A21.

Luik, John, "Bulletproofing Canada: Gun Control Won't Prevent School Shootings. But Having Guns Might Help Individuals Mitigate Them," *Western Standard*, May 21, 2007, p. 41.

Malkin, Michelle, "Wanted: A Culture of Self-Defense," Townhall.com, April 18, 2007. http://townhall.com/Columnists/MichelleMalkin/2007/04/18/wanted_a_culture_of_self_defense.

McManus, John F., "No Compromise Against Gun Control," *New American*, May 26, 2008, p. 27.

Milwaukee Journal Sentinel, "Schools and Guns: Ignoring a Key Ingredient," October 13, 2006. p. A22.

Nowicki, Ed, and David B. Kopel, "Ready to Shoot: The Legal Availability of Handguns Makes for a Better-Prepared Police Force and Safer Citizenry," *Baltimore Sun*, February 27, 2008, p. A11.

Ponnuru, Ramesh, "NRA Nation: The Second Amendment People Are Winning," *National Review*, August 13, 2007, p. 17.

Pratt, Larry, "Making Our Neighborhoods Safe: A Fearful Policy of Zero Tolerance for Firearms Does Not Provide Safety or Security; Only an Emphasis on Personal Responsibility over Government Dependence Can Do That," *The New American*, April 14, 2008, p. 17.

Robson, John, "Gun Bans Benefit the Violent Criminal," *Ottawa Citizen*, September 22, 2006, p. A14.

Rosenthal, John, "Make Federal Laws to Reduce Gun Access," *Boston Globe*, January 7, 2006.

Schwartz, Emma, "A Key Case on Gun Control," *U.S. News & World Report*, March 6, 2008.

Simon, Stephanie, "Guns Belong in Schools, Dealer Says; Online Seller Whose Products Were Used in 2 High-Profile Shootings Argues More Firearms Will Make Students Safer," *Chicago Tribune*, March 5, 2008, p. 4.

Stephen, Andrew, "The Unmentionable Causes of Violence," *New Statesman* (1996), April 30, 2007, pp. 20–22.

Stossel, John, "Guns Save Lives," Townhall.com, February 2008.

Stossel, John, "Myths About Gun Control," RealClearPolitics. com, October 19, 2005. www.realclearpolitics.com/ Commentary/com-10_19_05_JS.html.

Taffin, John, "Who Needs an Assault Rifle?" *Guns Magazine*, June 2008, p. 106.

Vatz, Richard E., and Lee S. Weinberg, "Any Lessons from Virginia Tech?" *USA Today*, July 2007, pp. 62–65.

Wellems, Bruce, "Too Young to Die," *U.S. Catholic*, April 2004, p. 50.

Williams, Byron, "The World Must Wonder How U.S. Can Tolerate Guns," *Oakland Tribune*, September 7, 2006.

Williams, Richard, "Shooting: Why Britain's Shooters Should Stop Whining About Pistol Ban," *Guardian*, January 17, 2006.

Williamsen, Kurt, "Beyond the Gun-Control Debate," *New American*, May 28, 2007, p. 17.

Web Sites

Bureau of Alcohol, Tobacco, Firearms and Explosives, U.S. Department of Justice (www.atf.gov/firearms/ index.htm). A law enforcement agency within the U.S. Department of Justice, the goals of the Bureau of Alcohol, Tobacco, Firearms and Explosives are to reduce violent crime and prevent terrorism. The Web site contains research, information, and publications about state and federal firearm laws and regulations, and statistics, including crimes involving young people, illegal gun trafficking, and firearms traced to crimes.

Doctors for Responsible Gun Ownership (www.claremont. org/projects/projectid.12/project_detail.asp). Part of the Claremont Organization, this organization is composed of health professionals familiar with guns and medical research. It works to correct poor medical scholarship about the dangers of guns and to educate people on the importance of guns for self-defense. The organization has legally challenged laws that regulate guns.

The Future of Freedom Foundation Gun Control Page (www.fff.org/issues/guncontrol.asp). This page, published by the Future of Freedom Foundation, contains links to recent anti-gun-control articles by a variety of authors.

JURIST, The Legal Education Network: Gun Laws, Gun Control, and Gun Rights (http://jurist.law.pitt.edu/gunlaw.htm). A legal news and legal research program of the University of Pittsburgh School of Law, the Web site offers an extensive overview about gun laws, control and rights.

Women Against Gun Control (www.wagc.com). This is a site by and for women. It argues that women need guns to defend themselves against crime, particularly rape and murder. The site contains information about why women should arm themselves and which politicians support and oppose gun control.

Index

Dunblane massacre, 33, 34
Durston, Bill, 24

E
England, gun control laws in, 14–15, 34
Europe
  gun ownership in, 14, 18–20
  murder rates in, 14, 17

F
Firearms. *See* Guns
Fox, James A., 31, 33
Friscolanti, Michael, 29

G
Gallagher, Mike, 8, 15
Gatehouse, Jonathon, 29
Germany, 14, 33
Gillette, John, 48
Greater good, 11
Greece, 14
Gross, Mikael, 46, 48, 50
Gun bans
  benefit criminals, 38
  ineffectiveness of, 20
  worldwide, 34
Gun control laws
  allow school shootings to occur, 44–51
  assault weapon ban, 27, 54–55
  can prevent school shootings, 52–56
  cost lives, 41–43
  do not stop criminals, 14–15

in England, 14–15, 34
public support for, 8–9, 27
recommended, 24–27
on registration and licensing, 24, 26
in U.S., 23, 34–36
weakness of, 55–56
Gun deaths, 22–23, 25, 27–28, 34
Gun lobby, 19, 24
Gun ownership
  causes violence, 29–36
  correlation between murder rates and, 14–20
  in Europe, 18–20
  prevents violence, 37–43
  restrictions on, 24
  as right, 7–11
  for self-defense, 19
  in U.S., 19, 35
Gun sales, private, 24
Gun technology, 9
Gun traffickers, 27, 54
Gun-free zones, 38, 50
Guns
  are not used in majority of crimes, 40
  endanger Americans, 21–28
  increase in number of, 16–17
  keep Americans safe, 13–20
  limit on bulk purchases of, 27, 54

Picture Credits

About the Editor

Lauri S. Friedman earned her bachelor's degree in religion and political science from Vassar College in Poughkeepsie, New York. Her studies there focused on political Islam. Friedman has worked as a nonfiction writer, a newspaper journalist, and an editor for more than eight years. She has extensive experience in both academic and professional settings.

Friedman is the founder of LSF Editorial, a writing and editing business in San Diego. She has edited and authored numerous publications for Greenhaven Press on controversial social issues such as oil, the Internet, the Middle East, democracy, pandemics, and obesity. Every book in the *Writing the Critical Essay* series has been under her direction or editorship, and she has personally written more than eighteen titles in the series. She was instrumental in the creation of the series, and played a critical role in its conception and development.